"Les Yong Brothers, deux acrobats de classe internationale, font inémir le public d'admiration… et d'inquiétude en exécutant une imposante série de tours de force et d'équillibre, avec cette splendide élégance qui n'appartient qu'aux meilleurs et qui a fait de ceux-ci, les vedettes du Lido de Paris."
~Gazette De Liege~

"…For some time now I have been receiving reports from abroad about their terrific feats, and now I have seen them in action….MIRACULOUS! MIRACULOUS!"
~London Daily Mail~

"Ein Balance – und Kraftfestival zeigen die Yong-Brothers mit Hand-und Kopfstandkunststücken in noch nie gesehener Art."
~DIE TAT~

"The amazing, fantastic performance of the Yong Brothers is the absolute highlight of a night full of spectacular."
~Chicago Tribune~

"Los Yong Brothers, un caso de fuerza y equilibrio sin precedents en el mundo."
~Informaciones~

A Balanced Life

Johnny Yong

the Peppertree Press
Sarasota, Florida

Copyright © Johnny Yong, 2011

All rights reserved. Published by *the* Peppertree Press, LLC.
the Peppertree Press and associated logos are trademarks of
the Peppertree Press, LLC.

No part of this publication may be reproduced, stored in a retrieval system, transmitted in any form or by any means, electronic, mechanical, photocopying, recording, or otherwise, without prior written permission of the publisher and author/illustrator.
Graphic design by Rebecca Barbier.

For information regarding permission,
call 941-922-2662 or contact us at our website:
www.peppertreepublishing.com or write to:
the Peppertree Press, LLC.
Attention: Publisher
1269 First Street, Suite 7
Sarasota, Florida 34236

ISBN: 978-1-936343-98-0

Library of Congress Number: 2011931252

Printed in the U.S.A.

Printed July 2011

To the memory of Tyrone

Acknowledgement

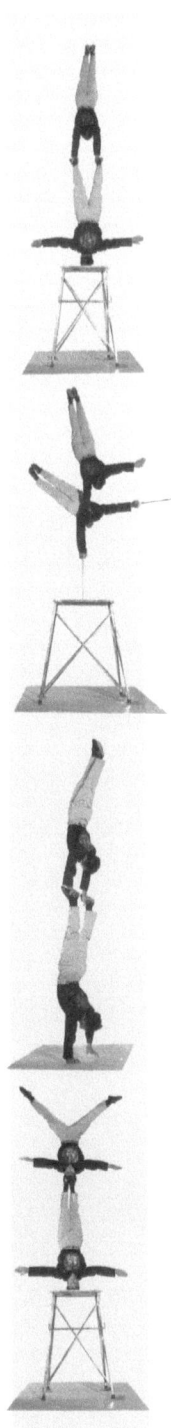

First and foremost, I want to acknowledge my great debt to Robert Van Praag who assisted me in putting my fond memories into words. Robert's tremendous writing skills enabled me to share the traveling experiences of *The Yong Brothers*. During the time we shared working on this book, Robert and I enjoyed our company together.

We forged a friendship that will endure for many years to come…Johnny Yong.

Prologue

"Are you really sure that a floor can't also be a ceiling?"

~M.C. Escher~

ADULTS OFTEN RECALL, OR POSSIBLY ASSUME SINCE they do the same thing, the many times that as children adults would look down at them (specifically the aunt who not only pinched your cheek but liked to mush it like silly putty) and ask in their imitation of a child's giddy voice their favorite opening sentence to a child who can't even tie their shoe laces yet, "So, what do *you* want to be when you grow up?"

As the child matures from four, five, to even six the answers go from cowboy, fireman, policeman, and then that wonderful time when their mothers get teary eyed as they say doctor.

Then there is the time that the child's imagination really goes wild after seeing a comic book, a parade, or talking with friends and announces to the world he wants to be in the *circus*! There is not a smile larger in the world than the time that the child screams the phrase he wants to be in the circus to a room full of laughing adults.

Then the laughter stops, the child's fantasies of trapezes, lions, and clowns fade yet somewhere in the back of his mind there is always that dream of, *"Wow, the circus!"*

No one ever stooped down to me (although my cheek is still bruised) and asked me, "What do you want to be when you grow up?"

My life was planned before I was even born.

The only thing that is unfortunate is that I cannot come up with a better phrase than "thank you." Of course, the appropriate question would be more akin to, "Why was I born so lucky?"

The dream that enters little kids minds and stays in the subconscious of all adults who manage to retain the gift of a child's innocence and fantasy for me was not then, nor throughout my life, a dream. More like a wish come true that I didn't even know I wished for.

What do I want to be when I grow up? The same thing I wanted when I was five, six, twenty, and forty…

…to be in the circus.

What *was* I when I grew up? *The same thing I was* when I was five, six, twenty, and forty…

…in the circus.

To children and adults I say dreams not only can, but do come true because dreams are only goals waiting for action.

My secret: A Balanced Life.

"It is possible to read upside down; it all depends upon how you see the world."

~Johnny Yong~

A Balanced Life

Chapter One

"Magic is believing in yourself, if you can do that, you can make anything happen."

~Johann Wolfgang von Goethe~

I BEGIN MY STORY WITH A COMPLETE TRUTH. One that many will not accept. Some because they do not believe it is possible. A lot because they do not want to face what they themselves did not possess.

I had a happy childhood.

And, much to the dismay of my mother's neighboring countryman Sigmund Freud, I loved both of my parents very much and I do not have any latent mother issues that need to be resolved.

Although I was blessed with a happy childhood, the one thing that to this day I cannot understand is that after traveling most of the world I have not found a single country who celebrates May 8, 1935 as a national holiday. I firmly believe it should be. It is my birthday.

If you can now accept that I am not lying in regards to my happy childhood, the next fact might make you again question your belief in me. I was born in Germany. Yes, in 1935; and I am being so bold as to tell you that I had a happy childhood; not regardless of the environment I was born into, but in spite of it.

My credibility gets tested further. I do not have any horror stories of the War. For me, it was entertaining. *No*, not as you think. Do not be ready to toss me aside as a Nazi and all that is associated with that word.

It was entertaining because I was, I am, an entertainer. One who was born into a horrible time and place where the concept of entertainment seems at the best, banal. At the worst, a sin. In many cases, a mortal sin.

I was a child; I lived in Germany throughout World War II. I am thankful that the atrocities that occurred during those years did not directly affect me. And, as distasteful as it might sound, all thoughts of the Third Reich as you view them need to be kept separate from my story, my life.

Unbeknownst to me, I learned something at this early stage of my life, a time when a child exists without complete understanding, which not only stayed within me but became the core basis for who I am. A child might not be a part (be that physically or shielded) of a war any more than a child might not be a part of a depression (ibid) but the effect it leaves upon them is a determinate part of their personality throughout their entire life

My father was born in China into a renowned family of acrobatic performers. On their own, they truly are legendary. My father traveled (performed) throughout the world and before he made his way to Germany was a feature act in the American vaudeville circuit where he performed with many of the greats including the master Al Jolson.

A regret right at the onset of my tale: I never had the opportunity to see him up on that stage; that never stopped me from seeing the star he was, learning from all that he offered, and the amazing talent he possessed.

He arrived in Germany and, as ironic as it might sound, fell in love with my mother in a movie theater. A sort of "life imitating art." Although I do not think what was on the screen had any relevance to the marriage of a Chinese man and a German woman.

With his love for the entertainment industry, his passion for making people smile, and his ties to the acrobatic arts in China my father not only created, but enacted, a plan for the entire family. A career. More importantly, a life.

He arranged for the *Namping Troupe*, an aspiring and gifted acrobatic ensemble of Chinese apprentices, to come to Germany where he would act as their director and manager. At the same time he began training my two elder sisters to follow in the family talent, legacy if you will, (the word "business" is far from appropriate) and at the age of five I joined my sisters in what was to become *"The Yong Sisters and Brothers."* (After the birth of my younger brother and my other "elder" [if one year can be considered older] sister entered the act.) I cannot recall at what age my father began training me, but I would not be surprised to learn that it began in my mother's womb.

While training and performing at that young age, I attended school. However, in 1942, I was forced by the State to leave. A child who was half Chinese and half German did not exactly fit into the Aryan standard of the government. While I had to wear identification on my clothing signifying my authenticity (although I would think it was rather obvious) I was not treated the way "others" who were branded by the government and forced to wear a label on their chest were. Furthermore, Germany held the same regulations that other European countries enforced.

My nationality (and hence my passport) was completely based upon my father's nationality, not where I was born. Hence, I was a German born child recognized as a Chinese citizen, from state papers to passport.

Little did I know that later in life this would be the cause of many, what might have been avoidable, *confrontations*.

I, out of school at the age of eight, was on my way to receiving the most miraculous education imaginable.

In the 1930's the *Kraft durch Freude* (Strength through Joy, *KdF*), a large state-controlled leisure organization in Nazi Germany and part of the German Labour Front was set up as a tool to promote the advantages of National Socialism to the people.

KdF was supposed to bridge the class divide by making middle-class leisure activities available to the masses.

When WWII began in 1939, one of the most important functions the *KdF* helped serve was to help setup and staff rest homes for German troops, provide concerts and entertainment for soldiers at the front, and help distribute amenities to traveling and returning men at railway stations.

Utilizing the most basic of comparisons, the *KdF* was the German version of the *USO*.

My family immediately became a part of the *KdF* and it was then that my true life as a performer, an acrobat, began into what would one day enable me and my brother to headline circuses, cabarets, lavish casino revues, and royal playgrounds.

I cannot tell a lie. If it were not for all of the newspaper articles and photographs I possess, I would wonder if all of the places I performed, and all of the people I performed with, were not a figment of my imagination; a childhood fantasy come true.

A Balanced Life

The fantasy that was more than a part of my life; it became my life in ignorance (for a five year old) of what was occurring around me.

Under the constant direction of my father I (we) preformed at hospitals for the recuperating soldiers, at the battlefront (as far away as Leningrad, although I would never know the horrors that took place in that city until much later) and in the cabarets of Berlin for the "entertainment" of the officers.

While the *Namping Troupe* was astounding audiences my father began bringing us into the act.

It was in these smoke filled cabarets filled with the stench of ale, and sights that my mother would not let me see, that I heard the most magnificent sound; the sound of two hands meeting together. The sound followed by the sight of actually seeing someone in the first row bringing their hands together to cheer...*for me*.

It is a sound that once it touches you stays in your soul for your lifetime. And after that first time, I was addicted to it.

My life was simple in structure; performing comes before all else. A training regiment of balance, timing, and strength. Yes, at the age of seven.

I was taught early on not only to strive to be the best that I could be, but, quite simply, the best. I have learned that the quality is not something to fear, but to be proud of.

The word "regiment" can be scary to some. In all facets of my life my parents were strict. But not the strict that one associates with bad, rather the strictness of parents who truly love their children and want only the best for them. I hesitate to say it, but the kind of strictness that lacks in present day society. A strictness – love – that inherently breeds respect into a child.

No one taught me not to yell at my mother or father. It was a given. A given that was one of the many moral principals I was raised with, and I thank them.

If the truth be known, which in fact it is by everyone I have ever worked with, I am far stricter on myself than my parents ever attempted to be.

The end of the War brought the realization – the horror – of what had occurred directly to my life – when I (we) returned home.

I was born in the town of *Goerlitz* which after the War was defined as East Germany; the allocated territory to the Russians after the dismemberment of Germany The Russian occupied forces did not treat the German citizens under their control any way near as bad as the Nazis had done to those under their control in lands that they had terrorized and seized, including the horrors that were purported about their debauchery of those Russians who had succumbed to them during the war.

Knowing that to be true, and knowing what "life" was like in *Goerlitz* for my family, I choose not to imagine (*cannot* imagine) what the Nazis had done to those that they had made subservient.

I was being persecuted (yes in hindsight, far too rash a word) for a war that I knew nothing of and never deemed to be a part of – and I ask forgiveness for my youth.

My family was in no way wealthy, but we could have been considered prior to the war, and then Russian occupancy, "comfortable." After the War the paper that money had been printed on was worth more than the money itself; at least paper could be burned for heat. My father had built a home for us where the first floor was for my grandparents, the second floor for our family, and the third floor was for my uncle. No, not grandiose, a place

– a home – for the family; and that meant the entire family.

Respect, not obligation. Desire, not guilt.

Our home, like the divided portion of the country, was now at the mercy of the Russians.

I do not need photographs to recall what poverty was like. And I do not think poverty is a harsh enough word.

Daily survival was a fact, not a concept. When the mere daily activity of eating is taken from you, when foraging for food is the only thing on your mind - that is the definition of survival. I cannot fathom the thought of actually having to see my children go hungry, starve to death, right in front of me; it makes starving seem preferable.

For my family, survival meant performing.

Somehow my father managed to get papers for the family to travel throughout West Germany as part of a circus. And yet I use the term circus hesitantly, as individuals congregating together striving to find any place to perform, a venue to give joy to people…*struggling to survive,* is not exactly the image of a circus.

And so my adventure began. In my young eyes I was part of a *caravan* as my family began on my first true experience in my life as part of the circus family. Performing anywhere there was a space that would hire us; a small theater, a cabaret, a mess hall filled with American soldiers. A life filled with traveling from city to city and, hopefully, bringing smiles (and in my case "oohs and ahs") to each village we passed through.

In my mind I think I can see us travelling throughout the country. When I pass a truck on the highway or I am at a gas station my memories come to life. The smell of diesel. The American troops travelled in trucks, we followed the troops. The smell of diesel. The smell of money.

Diesel fumes are not the only strong sense memory that I was left with from the war. One so small, yet so vivid. My sister and I would play in a *sandbox*. Germany had been infused with bombs. Bombs fall. Bombs leave their smells upon all of the land that they land on. Today I will be at a firing range or cleaning a gun for my present job and the memories of playing with my sister come back to me. Carbide. It should be a smell that conjures up images of death, to me, what many consider a rancid odor, brings a smile of my sister and I playing…in what we considered our *sandbox*.

From the end of 1945 through 1949 my father had infused in my blood the passion that his entire family had infused into him. My father's wisdom went beyond passion to reality. In a world faced by the uncertainties of war (he had already lived through two of them) as well as the practicality of families separating he wanted to insure that each of us had a specific talent that would be an act unto itself.

My eldest sister was a tap dancer in a time when tap dancing was at its height of glamour; a performing specialty that had the ability to leave the circus behind in favor of cabarets and theaters while audiences were clamoring for the sounds of those dancing feet. And, she was good. For a brother to say that his sister is good you can only imagine how talented she actually was. My other sister was a contortionist, what would one day be considered a master artiste of her trade.

And I was groomed into *hand balancing*. An act modeled after the renowned Unus, who was an inspiration and proud to say a friend for many years. At the time my brother was too young to be molded into his own talent and my "youngest elder sister" future acts had yet to be determined, but they assisted each of us in our performances.

A Balanced Life

I know I never knew, and I am pretty sure my father never imagined (knowing my father I could be quite mistaken), that it was not a matter of years - but months - that our individual specialties would combine us into a cohesive act that would literally bring us to stardom.

Again with relation to my opening statement about my childhood, I unequivocally give credit to my parents for what was about to happen; how they made it happen. Two parents who put their children above all else. My father training and guiding us every day, not as a tamer, but as a mentor and coach; but first as a father. And my mother, the strength behind all of us; a woman who recognized strength as much as she possessed it.

It wasn't until much, much later in life that I realized that I (along with my sisters and brother) was actually responsible for supporting the family. If I didn't realize it till much later it shows how important it was.

I had not been trained – given – a *trade*, but a *life*. Dare I say it, a magical one.

In 1950, upon request, we traveled to France to join *Le Bouglione Cirque d'Hiver*, the Circus of Winter Paris.

I thought I had made it! It had actually only just begun.

"Dreams are free, so free your dreams."

~Astrid Alauda~

Chapter Two

"Each player must accept the cards life deals him or her; but once they are in hand, he or she alone must decide how to play the cards in order to win the game."

~Voltaire~

PARIS. EVERYWHERE I TURNED THERE WERE BUILDINGS and monuments (what was left of them) to be explored, art on every street corner, people who held such elegance as they walked (as they liked to believe), and yet that is not the most powerful thing I remember about the city.

In a public room it came to me one day. I didn't see it. I didn't hear it. The most beautiful aroma I had ever sensed aroused me. I was a child during a war and I had been raised during the aftermath in a ravaged country; the smell that had me tingling: *pommes frites*. Forget the Louvre and the Eifel Tower - *pommes frites*. I knew I had arrived. More to the point, a smell that meant I had survived.

Don't get me wrong, I was fifteen; there was more to life than food (although many mothers would hesitate to agree.) And what is it that could be more important to a teenage boy than French fries?

The girls. Beautiful French ladies, and with them came a fragrance almost as powerful as the pommes frites: perfumes that to this day do not arouse me in the way they did then.

There was one other smell in Paris that was not unique. It smells the same all over the world; it is only called by a different name. The Metro, the Subway, the Tube…they all possess that stench of masses huddled together under the ground…but oh the places they bring you to.

At the beginning we stayed in cheap hotels where the bathroom served as our laundry and kitchen and the rooms were too small due to unwanted guests: fleas and bedbugs.

But outside was Paris.

And in Paris my mother warned me immediately to speak only English and Chinese, never German. If I faulted and a word of German came out of my mouth in front of the French I held their hatred. *Il m'a seulement pris six mois pour apprendre le français courant.* Fifteen and immersing myself in a new culture as I would many times over, that was education far more valuable than anything that I could have been taught in a tenth grade class room. I was too young to realize that, although it sounds trite, the entire world was going to be my classroom.

As it was the winter, the time when traditional circuses are dormant, we began by performing in clubs, cabarets, and any personal galas that we could be hired to entertain at. Other than that I practiced. I practiced with my body and with my mind. Always imagining what new feat could be performed, always ready to tackle yet another obstacle to become great, or, should I say, "One of the greats."

In March the season began and I found a whole new life, one that I had not imagined. For some it is an invitation to join the *Royal Shakespeare Company*. For some it is the *Bolshoi Ballet*. Right alongside them is an invitation to join the *Cirque Bouglione*, the *Cirque d'Hiver*.

All of the most famous acts including *Fratellini* and *Zavatta* performed with the *Cirque Bouglione* in a venue I had never experienced, to audiences that I had never fathomed.

And I was going to perform right along side these greats. Entertainers I am proud to call my friends. If I was thought to have the ability to be on the same marquee as them, if I could astonish the audience even half as good as them, then I had reached a level of success that, as an adult, I would have never thought imaginable; as a teenager, I undoubtedly expected.

On the bill of those performances was *The Yong Sisters and Brothers*. It was only a matter of months before we became a headliner in the show, an act with no rivals throughout all of Europe. It is one thing to have audiences salivate as you perform, it is something far more overwhelming to have the unfaltering respect of your peers.

The Yong Sisters and Brothers was an act with no competition. Hand to hand acrobatics at its best. It was said by those within the circus, those who saw our performances, and newspapers throughout the Continent.

And the better we got, the more respect we earned, the more my mind worked on improving what my body could master. There was a professional level to reach that I was determined to obtain.

In that first summer the act that was synonymous with *The Yong Sisters and Brothers* was revealed.

I balanced on my hands perfectly perpendicular to the floor straining my entire body as I pressed my entire torso into a thirty degree angle without moving so much as a centimeter from my hands' perfect vertical alignment.

The strength of the body was manageable, then came the strength of my mind as my sister did a handstand on my neck also staying perfectly vertical while her torso lowered into a twenty-five degree angle.

Me on the bottom, her physically, mentally, determined above me. This was followed by my brother placing his hands upon my sister's neck so that our three arms were all forming a straight line while he then managed to bend his torso and still position his legs straight up into the air. Me on the bottom, her balancing above me with her eyes focused down upon my scalp, my brother balancing on her neck looking though her neck to focus upon mine. A single unit.

It is easy for a spectator to view physical prowess; they had no idea the mental challenge was far more difficult then the pressure I was feeling in my arms. The test remained: what would collapse first – my mind or my body?

If you think this is hard to describe, imagine for a single moment how hard it was to achieve, the endless hours spent perfecting this acrobatic feat…the falls that happened along the way.

And on that night it began: Standing ovation from the crowd, actual applause backstage, and then the rivalry among agents, directors, and producers from throughout the European Continent for our attention, our time, our names on their marquees.

On that night we went from being *The Yong Sisters and Brothers* to being

THE YONG SISTERS AND BROTHERS

During the off season we performed at Christmas galas, cabarets and theaters throughout Paris and on one day the notoriety we were receiving all became crystal clear to me. It was not a cabaret that contacted us to perform, but it was at the request of the star performer that we were asked to share the stage.

The performer was Edith Piaf. A singer and cultural icon who became universally regarded as France's greatest popular singer and ironically began her career as an acrobat.

The praise, the star-status, that Humphrey Bogart and Lauren Bacall were receiving that same year on the screen (I take liberty but the analogy can be inferred), we had achieved in the circus and almost paled to now being recognized by the theater.

I relished in the Gypsy culture and the caravan lifestyle I had in the *Bouglione Circus* and our second season, 1950, brought us to Brussels.

The Korean War broke out and the panic seen on the streets in Brussels was mimicking that of the entire continent; the Americans had entered into war, the rest of the world would follow. Yet they came to the circus. They came to see all of the legends that were performing, they came to see *us*.

After another off season of performing again at galas and night clubs, we accepted an offer to join the Swiss *Circus Knie*, reputedly the most famous circus company and dynasty in Europe. It was while with this elaborate spectacular comprised of the most prestigious equine acts ever to grace a stage that I had my first chance to perform with *The Caroli Family*.

The *Caroli Family* can only be described as "your stereotypical, big Italian family" filled with love…and of course food! It was wonderful to be treated as one of their family; it was even better when they invited me to join them in a meal. I never learned how to cook from them, but I unknowingly learned how to speak Italian. *The world as a classroom*, or as I now knew, *Il mondo come un'aula.*

From the *Circus Knie* we joined Germany's *Circus Grock*, another one of the great European circuses. Although by this point we had the privilege of not working with any company but the best (please excuse the pretentiousness of what was a teenager speaking); *the best* is by whom we were requested for employment, we were a talent their audiences expected; would pay money to see.

Circus Grock was unique in that it was not a three ring (or one ring) spectacular but rather the entire performance was conducted on a rotating stage, providing a more theatrical, cabaret experience for the audience.

After one season with the *Circus Grock*, lest my passport feel neglected, we joined the Danish *Circus Schumann*, a circus founded upon the famed performers of the same name. It was with the *Circus Schumann* that I had my first honor of performing in front of royalty.

From performing on a battlefield, to sharing a room with fleas, and now to have royalty smiling and clapping their hands as I stared (for once I was gaping) at them while balanced upside down from center stage – and you might have had trouble believing me in the very beginning of my story.

1953 had me leaving the Continent and traveling across the channel to join the *Bertram Mills Circus*, performing at the Olympia. As told in a full page review in the London *Daily Mail*, December 1953:

> "...*Undoubtedly one of the finest balancing acts ever to come to this country is that of The Yong Sisters and Brothers. Their work is just out of this world.*
>
> ...*For some time now I have been receiving reports from abroad about their terrific feats, and now I have seen them in action.*

A Balanced Life

...a hand-balance on the feet of the bearer, who is in a free head-balance position...a one-hand balance on the neck of a bearer also doing a one-hand...then they build it up three high: our little top-mounter does a two-hand balance on the neck of his sister, who is doing a two-hand balance on the neck of the brother, and on a table too! In addition to this they do a free head-balance on the feet of the bearer who is also doing a free head-balance.

MIRACULOUS!

...But here is the limit: the young top-mounter does a two-hand balance on the feet of his brother, who is in a hand-balance, and then the bearer walks around the ring with the top-mounter in his hand-balance...MIRACULOUS! MIRACULOUS!"

It had not been the first time I had seen a review like this, it had not been the first time the audience had appreciated us so, but England was now accepting us the way the entire Continent had.

But that wasn't what was miraculous for *me*. My miraculous moment occurred when I found out I was performing in the same show as the *internationally* acclaimed circus star *Charlie Rivel*.

Please let me clarify. This was like a kid from the Bronx going from stoopball to playing with Babe Ruth! Charlie was beloved all over Europe, feted by royalty and popular audiences alike. And I was proud to call him my friend. He received every honor and accolade open to a performer. And I was honored to perform on the same stage as him.

My mouth was held agape once again when in the spring of 1953 *The Yong Sisters and Brothers* were requested for a *Royal*

Command Performance. It could have been my own opinion, but there is something completely overwhelming, almost mystical about asking to perform for *British* Royalty.

The most respected, renowned, and audience beloved circus performers throughout Europe always have one thing on their mind, and in the spring of 1954 it happened for me.

We were approached to join the greatest show on earth: *Ringling Brothers*.

In April of 1954 we left for the United States…to be a featured act in the *greatest show on earth*.

We were *asked* to join *the greatest show on earth!*

> *"Life is a great big canvas, and you should throw all the paint on it you can."*
>
> ~Danny Kaye~

A Balanced Life

Chapter Three

*"When you are not practicing, remember,
someone somewhere is practicing,
and when you meet him he will win."*

~ Ed Macauley~

I ARRIVED IN NEW YORK HARBOR WITH MY FAMILY the first week of 1954; *The Yong Sisters and Brothers* act ready to conquer the world. I was determined, convinced, that I would amaze the American audience the way we had the patrons in Europe.

My first day on land did not begin exactly as I had expected. There was a strike by dock workers and it was impossible to get our baggage off the ship. I am tempted to say that this set the stage for my initial impression of America for, in truth, the chaos at the arrival port mirrored exactly what I found in New York City.

I had traveled through all of the major cities of Europe, cities that I witnessed at the aftermath of war. They in no way compared to the chaos of New York. It would be wonderful to say I was in awe of the tall buildings and the thousands of people, but in fact it was just a state of erratic commotion; a place where an entwined mass of humanity seemed to exist as if each was alone.

The city held the friendliness of the inside of a lion's cage and didn't appear to have a tamer anywhere nearby. I had seen a lot. I was not naïve. But the city really was more than a mild shock, it was a disappointment.

On the ship there were some acts that had travelled with us from Europe and when I first met the performers at *Ringling* they had heard of us, made us feel welcome. But if that was the case, why did I still feel like a stranger. Not merely a stranger in a foreign land, but a stranger within the circus. The "new guy" in town. After years of knowing everyone I had performed with, literally growing up with friends that became families that I had either travelled (and ate) with or met again months later at a different circus, here I felt isolated.

The isolation didn't last as we had one week to practice before the opening night show in Madison Square Garden. The city and circus might have been new to me, practice wasn't. And I was going to wow the first American audience I performed for as we had the royalty of Europe.

I was not prepared for what I faced on opening night. Chaos – just like the day we arrived. To me it was an inexcusable poor definition for professionalism and the mystique that went with the circus; the mystique, the atmosphere requested and expected by royalty. The difference? It wasn't chaos to those who had been with *Ringling* for any length of time, only to me.

Ironically, I should have been in awe on opening night the way that I am now. Marilyn Monroe was going to lead the circus into the arena on a *Pink Elephant*. Of course she had no idea how to get onto an elephant and to say she was frightened would be putting it mildly. Assistants were yelling for help, ladders, something that would enable her to get astride the elephant (in reference to the elephant, I cannot say *pink* twice.)

I walked up, reached under her, and pushed her up on the elephant as if it was no big deal me having my hand on Marilyn Monroe's backside. As I said - no big deal - until I saw a picture of it later. I am not sure if this incident provides the basis (or an example) for *Gentlemen Prefer Blondes* or *Some Like It Hot*.

Along with Marilyn Monroe the show was being opened by Shirley Jones and Charlton Heston. All in all a star-studded spectacular. I should have been excited. At that point I probably was, what followed left me with anything but the thrill performing had always been.

When people use the term "it was like a circus in there" they are not referring to the entertainment, but a chaotic event. That is what Madison Square Garden was like. There were three rings with two additional side acts performing at once; audience members seeing different acts ending at different times, applauding whenever the act in front of them finished. I would like to say there was no attention span from the audience, but who could blame them? There was just as much of a "circus" going on around them. Souvenirs, popcorn vendors, and if that wasn't enough, those annoying, what should have been outlawed, flashlights that would twirl throughout the evening.

Could it be that I was expected to compete for the attention of thousands of eyes who couldn't focus on one performance but needed to adjust to five while at the same time searching for the right vendor to buy whatever trinket their child wanted?

It was a nightmare. While the European circus was a theatrical event, this had the atmosphere of a rowdy sporting event or a children's unattended playground. In addition, the American audience did not have the same appreciation for acrobatics that Europeans did; they wanted lions. It was not until much later when acrobatics became popular in cabarets, theaters, casinos, and even television, that the audience found their own sense of awe. Who knows, maybe we were too early – or maybe we provided the education – and, in any event (or conciliation), I was around for the realization.

One thing did change quickly though. I was immediately invited to all of the after show parties and socialized with many of the entertainers. I was beginning a "new family."

From New York we proceeded to the Boston Gardens, and then the life of *Ringling* began.

In Europe we spent a "week" in a city and moved on – to another city that was not far away in countries that are smaller than an individual state. My first month with *Ringling* can't be described, it has to be seen:

June 1	Atlantic City, N.J.
June 2	Newark, N.J.
June 3	Asbury Park, N.J.
June 4-5	Mineola, N.Y.
June 7	Stamford, Conn.
June 8	Bridgeport, Conn.
June 9	Waterbury, Conn.
June 10	Wallingford, Conn.
June 11	Worcester, Mass.
June 12	Springfield, Mass.
June 14	Albany, N.Y.
June 15	Glen Falls, N.Y.
June 16	Schenectady, N.Y.

A Balanced Life

June 17	Oneonta, N.Y.
June 18	Binghamton, N.Y.
June 19	Elmira, N.Y.
June 20	Geneva, N.Y.
June 21	Watertown, N.Y.
June 22	Syracuse, N.Y.
June 23	Auburn, N.Y.
June 24	Oswego, N.Y.
June 25	Rochester, N.Y.
June 26	Batavia, N.Y.
June 27	North Tonawanda, N.Y.
June 27	Jamestown, N.Y.
June 29	Youngstown, Ohio
June 30	I think I got vertigo or possibly what might be considered the forerunner of jetlag. And there were five more months in the season.

And I loved it.

The good thing? Performers, like in Europe, did not (actually were restricted from) take down or set up the tent and stages.

It did not matter how many towns we travelled through, how many performances we had in a day, every spare moment I practiced; always perfecting what we had, always coming up with new feats for the future. Two, three times a day– every free minute was dedicated to practice. *The Yong Sisters and Brothers* act was going to be as famous in America as we were in Europe. I might have motivated other performers to practice when they saw me, but I can guarantee that not one single act practiced as hard as I and my family did. And the proof was in the result.

At the end of the season, November, I migrated with most of the other performers to Sarasota, Florida, the winter home of

Ringing Brothers since 1927.

I stayed at *Southland Motel* owned by Unus, the phenomenal acrobat known for his finger balancing that I had known most of my life, and my time was spent either practicing or having fun on the beach. Really, imagine an acrobat prancing around on the beach- showing off if you prefer – it was a great winter. Sarasota might be known for its weather, but I am pretty sure that the girls on the beach would make a better brochure cover; the question being whether anyone would notice the aqua blue surfs being outshined by bikinis.

While in Sarasota on *winter break* we did travel for a show the first week of January, 1955 to Havana. Except for being a big shot and balancing on a pier where I ended up in the water that I didn't know was shark infested, Cuba was a great experience – from the treatment of Batista's staff to the rum that was given to the entire circus by the Bacardi family to take back to the States, which, if you didn't know, travels far better in animal cages guarded by tigers than in scrutinized suitcases.

While I might have *accidentally* fallen into the water with sharks in Cuba, back in Sarasota I was *thrown* to the sharks… by Mrs. Unus.

On January fourteenth I received a call that I was supposed to report to the beach the following morning by eight. Mrs. Unus had entered me into the *Mr. Sarasota* contest!

There I was on stage, literally hidden amidst these "massive" guys who were all oiled and posing and me, this "shrimp" among them not having a clue what to do. I tried to copy them and pose a few times, flexing my body the way they did, but let's face it – they were big – and I felt like a fool. Without going into an in depth description of the bodybuilders on stage, let me sum it up quickly by saying I am five foot six.

I guess it must have been instinct that got the best of me, because the performer in me took over. I dramatically lowered myself into a handstand – one handed and, to the applause that followed, I proceeded to "show off" my body with a few other balancing feats. Flexing without even realizing it.

Hold the drum roll please. I Won! *Johnny Yong, Mr. Sarasota.* And everyone in Sarasota soon new:

Main Street Reporter, January 21, 1955 – "

> *...joining our table was Johnny Yong of the famous Yong family. Nineteen year old Johnny was beaming with joy. He carried a large "gold" trophy which he showed us with great pride. He had won it in the Mr. Sarasota contest over approximately a dozen of "the best built" men in the city. Everybody greeted him with, "Hi Mr. Sarasota...and Muscle Man Yong."*
>
> *...Keeping in good physical shape is no problem at all to Johnny Yong and he has the muscles to prove it. Johnny is a "health seeker" and has reached his solid and glistening peak of near-perfection merely by working for a livelihood, believing his strength and muscular development comes from constant practice..."*

We spent the rest of the winter season in Sarasota and then went off for another "grueling" (wonderful) season with *Ringling* throughout 1955 and once again returned to Sarasota for the winter of 1956; a year of performing and practicing, followed by, sans bodybuilding, the glory of the beach. Performing, practicing, the beach; I agree with you, it was a rough life for a twenty-one year old.

By this point two of my sisters had married and the act was now *The Yong Brothers and Sister.*

1956 brought a drastic change to our schedule. Not by choice. On July 16th in Pittsburgh, Pennsylvania John Ringling, overwrought by a strike from the workmen who put the circus tents up, canceled the show, and not just the current tour.

He Closed the *Ringling Brothers Circus*. The show was to never perform again…at least under the Big Top.

It left us without work and my father immediately began hustling to find us bookings, utilizing any booking agents he could contact. We performed in the *Shrine Circus*, the Catskills with entertainers like Buddy Hackett and Alan King, went on to spend a month at fairs in Montana to be followed by small, week-long engagements as opening acts in Las Vegas.

Ironic, later in life when we were featured in Vegas I barely remembered those short stays.

It was then, in 1957, that Ringling decided to reopen the *Greatest Show On Earth, sans* the tent. In 1957 I was back to performing with *Ringling*. Going all the way from New York to California, stopping at "every state and town" in between!

Only a few years ago I received news from one side of the Atlantic that brought stars to my eyes; it was happening again in reverse.

In October of 1957 a European agent wanted to hire us to perform in Paris at *The Lido*, the club that since 1946 was the sparkle in the city of lights.

I do not know why, and I hesitate to think of the alternative, but *Ringling* let us out of our contract so what we could take the job, as a headliner act, at *The Lido*.

A Balanced Life

I was going back to Europe. To what I considered home. To what had made me into a "star."

My sister was going to remain with *Ringling* and it was my brother and I heading to Europe. Thus, the beginning of: **The Yong Brothers**

A suitable place for me to begin anew.

As we were preparing for the drive cross country to depart out of New York for France, the circus was getting ready to head toward their next location, for the next opportunity to bring smiles to kids in a town where the name would be forgotten long before the performers realized they were even there.

To many, racing across the country to meet a ship would seem like an adventure. To me, it was ordinary.

While I would be traveling across the ocean *Ringling* would eventually be making its way to a performance in Mexico City. As to the aforementioned "ordinary" trip across country, this is where *my adventure* began. A young couple from the circus had a two month old baby boy with breathing difficulties and they didn't want him to be in Mexico City where the elevation would put a strain on the boy. They were truly at a loss over what to do.

When they found out we would be driving across the country they asked if we would mind taking the child with us to Youngstown, Ohio where his grandmother lived. To those who have not had the privilege of existing in the circus environment, the circus is a family and all that is implied by that word. Of course I agreed. Before we left they insisted on giving me $75 to cover the cost of gasoline for the trip. It didn't exactly go that way.

While still in California I was pulled over for speeding. And thus, there went the money that was given to me. However, that alone would have been no big deal. When the highway patrolman was writing out the ticket he saw the baby in the backseat and asked my brother if the child was his. My brother, in an ignorant panic, said no. He then asked me, and after hearing my negative answer, would not give me the chance to explain.

Now in hindsight I have to admit, a twenty-two year old and eighteen year old travelling cross country muttering something about the circus and carrying a baby boy that wasn't theirs sort of gave the officer reason for brining us into the station. I was lucky that while we were being questioned at the station the officer was able to reach the grandmother in Ohio and confirm our story. I can only imagine the heart attack on the end of the line when the grandmother heard from a police officer in California about her grandson and two young guys – well, maybe I can't imagine it.

With that *experience* behind us we continued on our trip and made it *all the way* to New Mexico without incident. In between feeding, burping, and changing the baby (which always seemed to be at its dirtiest while I was in the passenger seat and my brother was driving), we got a flat tire. As I was changing the tire I looked out over the hills and I saw shadows growing in number. As I stared, I saw the shadows had cowboy hats on. I'm talking scary, threatening image, not rodeo.

I had my brother give me my handgun from the glove compartment (as a traveling performer, going through strange cities never knowing who or what you might encounter, carrying *protection* was a *necessity*, not a frivolity) and I was ready to protect the child as if he was my own. Strange, not anywhere near a father, yet I had the instincts. At any rate, we were able to high tail (New Mexico lingo) it out of there – and New Mexico, without stopping for as much as water.

I could go on about the crying and the constant smells, the

having to throw a dirty diaper out of the window during a rain storm that wouldn't allow us to stop only to see it landing on the windshield of the bus behind us, or even about the enjoyment it sometimes was to have a baby in the car, but the simple truth is we made it to Youngstown on schedule (yes, three days from San Diego to Ohio with only one ticket) and as we dropped off the woman's grandson it gave proof to the feeling of children are wonderful when they're someone else's.

The circus might be a family, but I was twenty-two and with two more days of driving I would be on my way to the *Lido de Paris* to perform with the *Bluebell Girls*.

To save me the embarrassment, please feel free to insert the appropriate comment that you think is going through my head as I talk (and dream) about the breathtaking *Bluebell Girls*.

> *"People who say they sleep like a baby usually don't have one."*
>
> ~Leo J. Burke~

Chapter Four

"Some of the world's greatest feats were accomplished by people not smart enough to know they were impossible."

~ Doug Larson~

LE LIDO DE PARIS, WITHOUT A DOUBT one of the most famous cabarets in the world, which is positioned on one of the most beautiful avenues in the world, and is most recognized for the gorgeous *Bluebell Girls*; and soon *The Yong Brothers*.

It had been eight years since the first time I arrived in Paris. I had thought the city was glamorous then, after rejuvenating from the War, it was beyond words.

The thoughts in my mind were the same as they were the first time, but my body was now of the age to "complete" some of my thoughts. Or at least I hoped. In essence, I was now aware of where (who) those marvelous perfume aromas emanated from. I had travelled throughout Europe and America; the *pommes frites* no longer held their attraction.

Eight years had flown by, and at the same time they felt like an eternity; I had gone from being in Paris as *The Yong Brothers and Sisters* to *The Yong Brothers*. To err without caution, nor embracing modesty, I had reached a level of stardom that I had not dreamed of years before, a level that I knew I would reach…with practice, and practice, and practice.

In 1950 my family stayed at a flea ridden, bed bug infested hotel. In 1958 my brother and I were staying on the *Champs Elyse*. I cannot say the hotel was much better, but it was the *Champs Elyse*. It was like saying you lived on *Park Avenue*. It doesn't matter if your room is a water closet in the basement with no windows, it is *Park Avenue*.

Performing at *The Lido* reminded me of my love for the stage and the ambience it created. I was back in front of audiences that truly appreciated the art of acrobatics and in a theater that respected the acts of the circus rather than the flashlights in their hands and the chaos of the five acts grabbing, or diffusing in most cases, attention.

Each night was a *performance*. Some days were an adventure that seemed as if they themselves should have been a performance, rather than a reality.

I was walking in the Montmartre district, an area that could best be described as Paris' "red light district", without giving thought as to my surroundings.

I stopped abruptly as I saw that the end of the street I was walking on had been blocked off. Ironically, what I should have noticed first was that the *gendarmes* on the street who usually carried side-arms and batons were now armed with machine guns. I quickly turned to go back to my hotel and saw that the entrance on that end of the street was blocked off as well.

1958 was the height of the conflict between France and Algeria for its struggle to gain independence and the *gendarmes* had blocked off the street to question any one that looked out of place (which was an oxymoron for that street); foreign, dark skinned, swarthy individuals who might be there due to the conflict, to insight unrest.

In my case, the latter might not be true, but the former would be hard to deny.

They were going from person to person checking papers and "taking in" anyone who looked suspicious. When an officer came to me I made the mistake of replying to his initial question in French; should I have talked to him in English what happened next might have been avoided.

He asked for my identification and I explained to him that I did not have my passport with me (unheard of in Europe) which was Chinese (red flag number one). He then asked me where in China I was born and I took it upon myself to further confuse him by telling him that I was born in Germany (red flag number two). Then I gave him the identification I did have with me: my United States Green Card (red flag number three). And of course red flag number four, which only convinced him further that I must be some sort of criminal (lunatic?) - I told him I was a circus performer working at *The Lido*.

He immediately put me in the truck with the other *suspicious characters* that were being brought into the police station for questioning and, in hindsight; I can't really say I blame him.

As they began finger printing me, questioning me, and filling in forms at the station I made the mistake of further trying to convince them of my story by talking in French (rather than English as per my U.S. Green Card) and insisting to these *gendarmes* who got ruder by the minute that I had to leave to go to the theater for that evening's show. To add insult to injury, the name of the show was *Prestige*; anything but the position I was in at the moment.

An officer finally agreed to call *The Lido* and, as it was the middle of the afternoon, the phone got answered by a maintenance worker who had never heard of me. I think this actually gave the *gendarmes* satisfaction that they had brought me in and were holding me – the

Chinese, German, American, French speaking circus performer.

With only a couple of hours to the show's opening a sergeant, who was probably sick of my pleading, agreed to call *The Lido* again and this time he spoke with someone who verified who I was.

As I raced to the theater I was mad, furious at their stupidity, angry at their rudeness. And I couldn't blame them one bit.

When our engagement at *The Lido* finished I was happy to be leaving the *gendarmes* behind me, not the *Bluebell Girls*.

Our next contract featured us with Spain's *Circo Americano* which travelled throughout Spain. Compared with *Ringling's* schedule I am not sure if "travelled" would even be an appropriate word.

Ever the enlightened individual, I made sure to have my passport with me at all times.

In the end of 1959 we were contacted by our European agent to return to Paris for a limited engagement at the *Theatre de Etoile*. The engagement began with an opening night gala for some of Europe's elite ranging from Charles de Gaulle to Aga Khan. The fact that we were a supporting act was irrelevant; the fact that we were requested to perform by the star of the show was not.

In truth, I do not think the term "star" justifies the woman highlighting the evenings' performance: *Marlene Dietrich*.

I had performed for royalty. I had performed alongside entertainers that make the term great seem minuscule. How does one appropriately describe sharing a stage with *Marlene Dietrich*?

Subsequently, how does one say without complete embarrassment (or with humility) that she would become just one of the many greats that I had the privilege of working with?

At the end of the engagement I had a *complete day* to rest before we moved on to Denmark to join the *Circus Schumann*. With memories of my "youth" filling my head, it was as if I was being invited back for a family reunion.

Circus Schumann wanted to promote the upcoming engagement, and my brother and I were the vehicle for promotion. I would like to say that I was engulfed with confidence over the forthcoming media spectacle and that my belief in my abilities replaced fear; some might say that I was bordering on the insane.

In the heart of Copenhagen, sitting just across from the Tivoli Gardens is the SAS (Scandinavian Airlines System) building with a view from the roof twenty-two stories above the city that was (for some) breathtaking.

The circus wanted promotion, my brother and I provided them with a full page story with a picture that made me think possibly the ones who thought me partially insane were correct. I did a handstand, my brother proceeded to do a handstand balanced upon my neck, the crowds were in awe – on the ground twenty-two floors below us - as we balanced on the *edge* of the building.

The photo in the paper suggests that no one should have thought I was unbalanced (mentally this time) with the possible exception of my brother for trusting me with his life *balancing on the edge.*

After only six months we were contacted by *Ringling* to return to the States to join them for the 1961 season.

Twenty-five years old and my life was already a state of déjà vu.

What occurred next was not déjà vu, nor do I want to ever experience it again.

When we got off the boat in New York and I proceeded through immigration I was told that I had to immediately report – within twenty-four hours - to the nearest draft board.

> *"The question isn't who is going to let me; it's who is going to stop me."*
> ~Ayn Rand

Chapter Five

"If opportunity doesn't knock, build a door."

~ Milton Berle~

MY FEARS WERE NOT OF WHAT I MIGHT ENCOUNTER while in the army, my fears were of all that I was leaving behind should my name get called for enlistment. And it wasn't a case of "should"; it was a case of "when."

Two years without performing. Then I got devastated. If I returned from the army after two years it meant that my brother would probably be drafted shortly after my return. Could the act last after four years of us being apart? If it could, would anyone care?

We made the decision that my brother would enroll with the draft board the same time I did so that at least we would only be apart for two years. Ironically, this wasn't necessary. Due to a physical ailment that had stayed with my brother since birth, when he was x-rayed the government found him ineligible to be drafted. That left a "possible" two years without us performing – practicing – our act. Call me stupid; it was not going to alter my career – my life – at all. Two years were going to be an intermission to me in-between acts; not a finale.

I was performing with *Ringling*, different day – different city – when after six months I received my orders from the government. On August 4, 1961 I was inducted into the United States Army.

I had a friend who was in the intelligence department of the army and I was hopeful that he would be able to "pull some strings" and have me placed within that department as well. In addition, I was sure the value of being fluent in four languages would make me an asset to the intelligence department.

It was not to be.

After boot camp I was sent to *Fort Carson*, Colorado for infantry training. I would like to say this is where my harsh life as army personnel began. I'm not sure it would be exactly fair to say that. At *Fort Carson* I was assigned as a lifeguard to the pool. Really, a lifeguard.

While I "struggled" in the morning doing my lifeguard "duty" I also managed to get a job as a lifeguard at the *Broadmoor Hotel* for most afternoons. A soldier with a tan.

In addition, I was performing weekends at the *Pampam* nightclub near the base of Pike's Peak. Lifeguard during the week, entertainer on the weekends earning $200 a week. The army.

My papers were supposed to be marked as "special personnel" meaning that I would not be called away from *Fort Carson*. I stress the phrase *supposed to be*. I returned to the base one day after a hard afternoon of lifeguarding and looked at the bulletin board only to find that I was being called overseas.

I was thrilled. Back to Europe. In a way, back home. Wrong.

I was being sent to the Pacific, to Korea.

Dreading being sent to Korea I talked with a soldier who had recently returned. He told me to turn the bad into good. There was a lot of money to be earned in Korea. To put it in simplistic terms, he told me there was money in "banking." The advice I was given was rather obvious. He told me to bring as much cash with me as I could to Korea and then I could lend it out to other soldiers. Let's not forget, most soldiers were a few years younger than I was where their only concerns with money were for fun. In Korea that meant prostitution (where the prostitutes outnumbered soldiers twelve to one), drinking, and gambling (not necessarily in that order.)

Once off the plane, I found an even more lucrative banking opportunity.

U.S. soldiers were paid in military scrip. It was in effect the military form of currency, not dollars. As such, when they were off base they would pay for any "activities" they indulged in with scrip This is where it got tricky. Soldiers would pay the local Koreans in scrip. To the Koreans it was useless; they were not allowed to change it into dollars on the base and had virtually no where to spend it freely. They had to find a way to "launder" their scrip. Enter "the bank."

I would take one hundred U.S. dollars that I had brought with me and trade it to the Koreans for seven hundred dollars worth of scrip. Seven to one exchange! I would then take the scrip and loan it out to the soldiers, who would ironically probably end up spending it with the Koreans if they didn't gamble it away. Anyway you look at it; I was "a bank" - taking money in and loaning it out - and a very profitable one at that.

Business enterprise aside, being in Korea could only be described as far from pleasant. However it was not until later in 1962 that *fear* truly entered the atmosphere.

1962. The Cuban Missile Crisis. The erection of the Berlin

Wall. The fear of war. Democracy versus Communism. Korea.

As a sniper in Alpha Company, we alternated being stationed in the DMZ. My rotation arrived just as the world was gripping these horrible occurrences. I am not embarrassed to say I was scared $#%@ to be heading into the DMZ.

Until my deployment (scheduled rotation) into the DMZ I, along with all, had trained with non-live ammunition. This was not going to be the case. On my first assignment I was stationed in a tree as a lookout. Rifle in hand, I found myself looking out through my scope at the countryside, small animals or shadows. Almost daydreaming rather than scoping out any enemy presence.

I lifted the scope to my eye and as I looked out I became paralyzed as I saw a sniper in a tree no more than a few hundred yards from me looking directly back at me through his scope.

Was it lack of training that left me inert, confusion over the snipers presence, or pure fear that held me still? I don't know. What I do know is that rather than shoot I fell from the tree. Landing on the ground I grabbed my rifle, and when I looked back at where the other soldier had been positioned, the tree was empty. There was no sight or sound. In truth, I had just been faced with an opponent who was no more prepared for what he had seen than I was, and assuredly just as petrified.

Back in camp I laid on my cot still shaking saying a prayer of thanks…and a prayer that the situations in Cuba and Germany would have the same results so that I could get back to *fake* bullets.

With the exception of my brush with death I stayed in shape, I practiced whenever I could; I had a career – a life to return to.

"Choose a job you love,
and you will never have to work a day in your life."
~Confucius~

A Balanced Life

Not only did I perform for men in my unit, but I also "took my act on the road" and did shows at other nearby camps. Johnny Yong, one man USO! Maybe not performing for royalty, but in many ways it felt better. And not to downplay the trophy I received for being Mr. Sarasota, but in 1963 I won another one: "All Army Entertainment – Individual Specialty!"

Then the real USO came to town – complete with Bob Hope. I had worked with Bob on a few occasions (Vegas and State Fairs) and when he saw me he asked me if I would like to perform with his act in Seoul performing a skit with Lana Turner. Forget about pinups on your locker…a skit with Lana Turner!

When the evening was over Bob asked me why I was in Korea. I'll let you supply my answer. He told me that he wanted me to finish the USO tour with him and when I explained that I couldn't he went to talk with my commanding officer.

Twenty four hours later I was on tour with Bob Hope, Lana Turner, Anita Bryant, Tommy Dorsey, and, well you get the idea. Twenty-four hours from solider back to performing with stars! There is such a thing as karma…and connections…and clout.

After we entertained in Japan and Hawaii we returned to the States, where on July 12, 1963 I was discharged from the army in Fort Lee, Virginia.

I didn't return with any medals, but I had a trophy, a kiss from Lana Turner, and the honor of knowing my friend Bob Hope had *recruited* me *from* the army for his show.

"If you want to make your dreams come true, the first thing you have to do is wake up. "

~J.M. Power~

Chapter Six

"The world is a book, and those who do not travel read only a page."

~St. Augustine ~

DURING MY FIRST WINTER SEASON IN SARASOTA I encountered many beautiful women. I had only fallen in love with one of them.

Upon my discharge I went north to Boston where my beloved Astrid was performing her hand balancing feats in a cabaret. Astrid, a North Germanic name meaning *"divine beauty"* – and when her parents named her they must have been inspired.

We were married in Dartmouth, New Hampshire and while my wife (wonderful word) stayed in Boston to finish her contract I went to San Francisco to be with my brother and *resurrect* our act. I would like to say it was twenty-four hour days of practicing; it felt more like thirty hour days. As far as I was concerned they could have been forty-eight hour days, eight days a week.

Walter and I travelled for three weeks performing at any location that had availability, hastening to renew our act, and in a short time we landed a job in San Francisco's landmark cabaret *Bimbo's*; named after the owner, not the patrons or the cast. While there we were contacted by *Ringling*. And albeit the skepticism from a media convinced that we could never "make it back – never be as good as we used to be", we not only got our old routine back and perfected, but improved upon it during our entire 1964 season with *Ringling*.

It was then back *home* to Sarasota when the season ended.

The New Year brought new excitement into my life as *The Yong Brothers* along with my *very* pregnant wife went to Reno to perform in the *Hello Tokyo Revue*. We had only been there for a few weeks when Astrid returned to Florida as birth of our first child was imminent and she wanted to be with her parents. To be succinct, regardless of her commitment to work, and our love which wanted us to be together, bringing life into the world while on the road is not exactly the ideal scenario.

It was then that the beauty and the disaster of yin and yang entered my life when on February 26th my daughter Tina was born and shortly thereafter the hotel where I was performing in went bankrupt; Goodbye to the *Hello Tokyo Revue*.

It was back to Sarasota with no chance of securing any entertainment work that "late" in the year (as far as booking went.) As such, I was forced to take a "job." I worked at it with the dedication of any commitment I had made, but it was a "job." Nine to five that can only be summed up as boredom. Fortunately that left many hours for practice…and my new daughter.

Towards the end of the year I was contacted by our European agent and we spent three months in front of the television camera on variety shows in Germany, Belgium, France, and Spain and as thrilling as that was, never seeing the delight of an audience (or hearing their hands meet) was more of a disappoint than the

A Balanced Life

thousands who would be viewing us from their living rooms.

As usual, come December I was back in Sarasota, not that I would ever complain about spending the holidays with my precious little gift on her first Christmas, and at the beach no less.

Although a few weeks late, I received a gift *almost* as dear as my daughter, when in January of 1966 I became a United States Citizen. Ironically, the moment I became a citizen it was time to leave the country again. To someplace completely new to me, some place, after all of my travels, which I could call "foreign." Lebanon.

Unbeknownst to many, there is a casino resort in the world that makes the ones in Las Vegas look like a Motel 6. Perched atop a cliff overlooking the Mediterranean is the *Casino du Liban*. A hotel with the atmosphere of luxury, refinement, and a sense of excellence that are the essence of *Casino du Liban's* myth and was on the itinerary of the international jet-set throughout the 60's and 70's. Needless to say, the state-of-the-art showrooms matched the elegance of the golden chandeliers you saw when entering.

I can't say I actually rivaled the linen cloaked sheiks and tuxedo clad James Bond look-alikes that partook of the *Casino's* indulgence once they stepped off the cable car that brought them up the side of the mountain to the *Casino's* doors, but my family and I were treated like royalty as far as I was concerned.

Staying in Jounieh at my beautiful villa on the beach, complete with a housekeeper, I was steps away from the blue waters of the Mediterranean. Unfortunately the beach was just as inviting as the sea and I spent so many hours in the hot sun that on one evening I ended up, much to the astonishment of my co-workers, performing with heat stroke. Let me be clear; walking around the stage on my hands with my brother balanced above me with heatstroke. Was I delirious after the heatstroke or before remains to be seen; it is irrelevant when you work in a profession that is ruled by the phrase, "no work, no pay."

Every moment of my life seems to have been filled with unexplainable occurrences. I had a cousin living and working in Lebanon, in Jounieh, who read in *Casino* advertisements the announcement about the appearance of *The Yong Brothers* in their upcoming show, and contacted me upon my arrival. Me, this German born, Chinese nationalist, now an American citizen meeting a cousin in Lebanon. I choose not to try to understand it.

My villa came complete with a landlord who was literally a fish fanatic who insisted on sharing his bounty with me and my family. The repetitive repugnant odor of the fish combined with the less than wonderful stench of goat or lamb that abounded every corner were enough to have me wondering if camel was edible, or at least if it smelled better. Fortunately, I did not have to go to this extreme.

Performers at the *Casino*, knowing my *thirst for real meat*, told me about a butcher that was in the downtown, old area of Beirut. Not the kind of place to wander into, but a butcher! The first couple of times I ventured there I took a taxi on my own for the ridiculous cost of twenty-five dollars – yet it was worth it. I then found out that there were "group taxis" that piled six, seven people on top of each other where the cost would only be $2.75. Twenty-two dollars for more sausages. If the driver knew I was a foreigner I would have been taken advantage of so I spoke French.

By the fifth trip I got even wiser to the treatment I received as an "outsider." I dressed up, barely able to recognize myself in a mirror, like a Muslim. I held a pretense of being mute in the cab avoiding disclosure and all went fine on the trip to the butcher -- and then came the return.

While my overflowing bag of sausages and cutlets was at my feet we were stopped at a roadblock by soldiers with machine guns…looking for sausages? It was as good a guess as any for I never found out why we were stopped. At any rate everyone had their hands up showing papers and before I could show my American passport (and afraid to let on to the others in the taxi that I could speak) someone started screaming about the *contraband* meat in the car and pointing at me.

I suddenly began speaking in French to the soldier who was beside me and explained to him that I was with the *Casino du Liban*. The soldier saluted me. I would like to say he had some awe about my being a performer there, in truth he was probably in fear of the fact that I worked for a government owned entity. I then showed him my American passport and he once again saluted me. When I told him where I lived in Jounieh he insisted on taking me back to my villa urging me never to engage in an act like this again, not out of the law but out of fear for my life.

Things were going wonderful for two months and then on June 5, 1967 a war broke out that the world would hear about for decades to come, and as guns were firing in the distance (close distance) all hell broke out on the streets of Lebanon. The American embassy immediately contacted me and "gave me" and my family twenty-four hours to leave the country. We were being evacuated. Gather our papers and any irreplaceable items that we could carry, report to the embassy, to awaiting American airliners, and leave the country.

We arrived in Athens almost penniless, save for what was now worthless (to me) Lebanese pounds. It was thanks to a businessman there that I was able to unload a vast amount of Lebanese pounds (at a great loss) in exchange for $1000...and our lives.

From Athens we proceeded to Paris not only near broke, but without all of our equipment – our livelihood - that we were forced to leave at the *Casino*. I do not question how he managed to do it, but my cousin was able to secure all of our belongings from the *Casino* and eventually shipped them to me in Paris.

As fate seemed to have a way of intervening, I was only in Paris a month before we were once again contacted by *Ringling*. To say that the circus is a small world with large ears would be to put it mildly. Not only small, but everlasting. While waiting for our engagement with *Ringling* I haphazardly met on the street a member of the Bouglione family who remembered me and told me if there was anything he could do to help us through our current situation, to contact him immediately. Unless I am mistaken it had been almost fifteen years since I had worked with the *Cirque Bouglione*. Family.

Ringling was participating in a cultural exchange program with Russia and we were on our way to meet them in London in order that we could all travel together to Moscow.

Russia had an amazing respect for acrobats of all kinds and we were treated not only with respect, but admiration. Lest you think my life had gotten boring, I share with you the debacle I faced in Russia, which seemed to be an occurrence wherever I traveled.

The members of the circus had been assigned a KGB agent to "protect" us. On the day of the evening of our first performance I returned to my room only to find that my personal papers, passport included, had been taken from my briefcase. Not misplaced, absconded.

In an absolute fury I informed "our" KGB agent what had happened and insisted that if my papers were not returned to me I would not go on that evening.

Prior to the performance my papers had not been returned to me and I think it was a good thing that I went on stage, if only to prove me innocent, of what I did not know, they suspected. In addition, I would have missed the amazing experience that occurred when we first took our positions on the stage; the audience began applauding loudly, throwing flowers and candy…all before the performance…a standing ovation in advance.

When I returned to my room my papers had been placed on top of my briefcase – along with my passport which answered all of my questions and was the source of my dilemma.

The photo on my passport was one of me in my army uniform. They had assumed (thought that I might have been, were taking precautions?) I had entered the Soviet Union as a soldier, not a performer, until I had the good sense (more likely luck in my case) to go on stage that night.

The opening night gala for government officials in Moscow was followed by eight phenomenal weeks performing throughout Russia. It was wonderful to be treated so warmly. It was wonderful to be treated with such respect. It was astonishing to be in a country that treated our entertainment as an art.

In 1968 I was back in Paris…without a criminal record…again.

> *"If you reject the food, ignore the customs, fear the religion and avoid the people, you might better stay home".*
>
> ~James Michener~

King Constantine of Greece, Princess Ann Marie of Denmark, Princess Alexia, and Tina Yong

Chapter Seven

"To dare is to lose one's footing momentarily. To not dare is to lose oneself."

~ Soren Kierkegaard ~

I DON'T KNOW IF PARIS WAS A PLACE I MERELY RETURNED to at an end or a place where things began anew. Once again we were back to hustling for engagements, performing in cabarets whenever there was availability. The schedule kept us on the road, and on an occasion when we were appearing at a theater in Geneva the most memorable event, or relevant in an abstract way, was that I bought a portable typewriter. No applause please. However, it proved its value upon my return to Paris.

I was at the *Claridge Hotel* waiting to meet Kate Bronnet, the owner of the famed Swedish *Cirkus Scott*. While I was awaiting her arrival I saw a gentleman near the phone I recognized as one of the *Ink Spots* who I had performed with back in the States. I went over, slapped him on the back and, much to my astonishment, when he turned I found out it wasn't an *Ink Spot* I had the misfortune to leave my hand impression upon.

To my horror, I quickly was informed that I had just slapped Sugar Ray Robinson across the shoulders. It does not matter if you have ever "struck" a world class fighter, you can imagine my surprise. And, I dare say, you have never met a kinder, friendlier boxing champion – even though I had just "hit" him.

With my new typewriter by my side, no I don't know why, and a smile from my recent introduction into boxing, I met the kind, talented, and professional Mrs. Bronnet. I think I have just used the term professional too lightly. After briefly negotiating a contract for my brother and I, and the expectations of being a member of her cast, Mrs. Bronnet told me I should "break in" my new typewriter right then and there and we could write and sign a contract immediately. It was my first typewriter; I don't know if "immediately" was the best term as I hunted for the keys. At any rate, *The Yong Brothers* were on their way to Sweden as a featured performance.

While the circus travelled from location to location via train, Mrs. Bronnet preferred to make the journeys by car. On many occasions I had the privilege of driving her; I say privilege because it was an honor to spend time talking with this woman I admired and, I quickly found out, was somewhat as free spirited as I was.

We stopped along our way for gas and when I mentioned money she told me she didn't have any on her so I should get some out of the trunk. I did not realize that the trunk did not hold her purse, but a bag with the previous days' receipts in it. When I simply placed my hand in the bag I had no idea how many bundled packets of bills I was touching. I'm talking thousands of dollars just sitting there in a duffle. I never realized how many hands were clapping during the previous couple of days, not to mention the fact that she thought nothing of riding through the country with a car trunk taking on the role of a bank vault!

Now, back to the more predictable Johnny Yong.

I was waiting outside of the hotel for Mrs. Bronnet for the drive to the next location when I was approached by the police. (I told you, predictable.) They explained that the box-car adjacent to the circus train was robbed and the thieves made off with a bunch of television sets and I was a suspect. What they expected me to do with a train car full of television sets or where I had carried and hidden them I had no idea. The situation was actually rectified rather quickly (not so predictable) when I showed them my passport – American passport.

The signature on my passport, which had been verified when I entered the country was, well, rather unintelligible. They were looking for a Jonny Song, not Yong. In truth, my "Y" does look like an "S". Without a trip to see what a Swedish police station looked like, they apologized and I took note of practicing my penmanship.

With my American passport came American pride. When July Fourth approached I asked the *roust abouts* (actually what one might consider "migrant workers" as they changed from city to city where the circus encountered "individuals" who would do anything for a buck) who were responsible for putting up the tent and stages, to place a United States flag on top of the tent to honor the holiday. When they complied, after a *gift* of some beer, and the circus manager saw the flag, the manager insisted they take it down. Mrs. Bronnet walked by and when she heard the disturbance insisted that the flag remain atop the tent.

I am not sure, but I think that was the first (and possibly only) time that July Fourth was honored in Sweden. And in essence, it was an honor given from Mrs. Bronnet to me.

Following the end of our stay with *Cirkus Scott* it was back to the United States (unfortunately for me there was no such thing as frequent flyer programs back then) and in 1969 we began touring with fairs, the *Shrine Circus* and *Hubert Castle Productions* where we found ourselves touring Montana, home to one of the country's most amazing national parks and "pic-i-nik" baskets.

Imagine a group of covered wagons all arranged in a circle at night by the wagon master for protection. Now imagine a group of circus motor homes and trailers all gathered in a "makeshift" circle, the closest thing that large mobile home trailers could fathom, by the ring master not for protection, but for an evening of fun complete with a camp fire, a barbeque tempting you with burgers that hadn't even reached the rare stage yet, a little "too much" beer, music, and blasting fireworks (of which the circus was in no short supply of) and that was how I spent July fourth, 1969 with my family at *Yellowstone Park*. More precisely, both my families; my wife and daughter, and the performers I shared my life with.

Children have these dreams of running away to the circus or living vicariously through a fairytale. I was in the circus fulfilling the former, and what happened after I "stumbled" into my trailer to sleep after the smoke from the fireworks faded, brought me into an actual fairytale, and not vicariously, fulfilling the latter.

I was awakened by a loud noise and when I looked out the window I saw this giant black bear. At his side was "Mama" bear (giant in her own regard) and at her heals was the cutest little "baby" bear. Naturally, being the intelligent individual that I am, I was curious.

In my "rational state of mind" I grabbed a loaf of bread and went out to feed the bear family. Not tamed, circus animals used to interacting with humans, but these wild foragers who had stumbled into our circle that I thought were cute and hungry... for bread no less.

When I stepped outside I called to them in German, there is something about the forcefulness of the language that animals (and humans?) respond to. They stopped (halted?) and when they turned I first began feeding the "Papa" and then offered a piece of bread to the "Mama" who was quite "civilized" until I offered a slice of bread to her baby. Amid her growling, and making sure she and "Papa" were munching away, I bent and started feeding "Baby" bear. (Need I remind you again, wild animals, not pets or circus talents.)

"Baby" bear was clutching my leg, almost cuddling against me, as I fed him and although the entire family wanted more to eat I walked over to a friend's trailer (as if this was an every night occurrence) and asked him for some aspirin. Amazing, I'm in the middle of three bears that could rip me to shreds in less time than it took to knock on a door and I casually went to get some aspirin. (I blame the fireworks, not the beer.)

With the bear family following behind me, and my friend in shock in front of me, I gave the bears the last of the bread I had and told them, again in German, that they needed to leave. I cannot be sure (or know why), but I think I was being polite while I was being forceful. The bears turned, and then casually walked away...without having slept in any beds.

The next morning all of my friends were yelling at me, telling me how crazy I was, and I acted as if "my evening with the bears" was no big deal. What is the scariest is that I actually thought so. The news travelled throughout the entire circus community and it seemed wherever I travelled to in the country people had heard of my wild (they probably preferred the word stupid) escapades.

In 1970 I went back to Europe and never heard any repercussions from my counterparts, many who I had known most of my life, about my little "bear adventure." Not that they hadn't heard the story, they were just probably not shocked by me doing such a thing. Is that good or bad?

It was Copenhagen again, this time without balancing my brother and me and like a flagpole on top of a building, as we joined the *Circus Benneweis*.

A truly unique experience for anyone who had ever spent their life in the circus, the *Circus Benneweis* was in a <u>permanent building</u> near Tivoli Gardens. No travelling at all for the entire engagement. While this was the case when performing in theaters and cabarets, a circus that remained in one place was like a miracle!

Circus Benneweis began with a spectacular water pantomime show complete with frolicking sea lions and alligator wrestling (not at the same time.) The fountain itself was run by a giant generator in the back of the building with a water tank that was, for simplicity, a barrel sealed by cables and screws – a barrel the size of a two-car garage.

After opening night we were celebrating and we heard a loud explosion. A few seconds later, what seemed like hours, we found out that the tank had burst; water was rushing out and heading its way into the basement. While our immediate concern was for any circus equipment that was below, we came to find out that it was paraphernalia stored for the winter when the facility was used as a movie theater, not our belongings. Regardless, the "dam" had burst and something needed to be done.

Manfred Doval, a renowned high wire aerialist, was first on the scene and began taking action before others even comprehended the damage. Due to his experience with rigging cables he immediately assessed the damaged and realized that after one cable had burst they all did. While Manfred, Walter, and I began fixing the tank the fire department was called to pump away the water.

However my experience in Denmark did not end on a wet note. (My apologies.) King Constantine, Princess Anne-Marie, and young Princess Alexia had come to see the show and, while not only astounded and overjoyed at the performances, they also remained afterwards for us to meet them; more importantly, for them to meet us. And for me, the coup de grâce was the expression on my daughter Tina's face when she presented them with flowers.

In America the concept of meeting and being praised by royalty might seem banal, in Europe it was an honor; and an honor for me to see my daughter standing with them.

Far more priceless than frequent flyer miles, which I hadn't even begun to accumulate…

> *"Success isn't a result of spontaneous combustion.*
> *You must set yourself on fire."*
>
> ~ Arnold H. Glasow ~

Chapter Eight

"Don't aim for success if you want it; just do what you love and believe in, and it will come naturally."

~ David Frost~

AS MUCH AS THIS COMES COMPLETELY AS A SHOCK, when the season ended in Copenhagen we went back to Sarasota for the winter; a warm, relaxing time to play with my daughter at the beach and celebrate the holidays with snowmen made out of sand.

After only a couple of short weeks my "holiday" was interrupted, but it was the farthest thing from unfortunate. When I managed to pull my tongue off the floor after speaking with my agent, I informed my wife and Walter that *The Yong Brothers* were asked to perform at *Radio City Music Hall* during the December, 1970 holiday spectacular.

I hesitate to use the phrase "asked to perform" and using the word "privilege" doesn't even come close to the honor. For any entertainer delighting audiences at *Radio City* is a dream come true. For a circus performer, even one who had traveled the world appearing at the most majestic casinos and night clubs, *Radio City* was a dream that could not even be imagined.

It made the thrill of *Madison Square Garden* seem minimal. It made the elaborate theaters of Paris seem less impressive. It made the grandiose casinos of Lebanon less awe inspiring.

It was *Radio City Music Hall.* A venue with no adjectives to describe it, and *The Yong Brothers* were going to be on its stage.

Radio City was a palace - the largest indoor theater in the world – constructed for the people who graced its doors, not its stages, albeit in my opinion those who had performed on its stages were worthy of a palace. A place of beauty offering high-quality entertainment at prices ordinary people could afford. A place where the audience was not only entertained and amused, but elevated and inspired to feel like the royalty I had been honored by in Europe.

Even before rehearsals began, I stood in awe of the Grand Foyer, the three mezzanines overlooking the orchestra, and the stage framed by a huge proscenium arch with a shimmering gold stage curtain that was the largest in the world, the masses of people that this theater could accommodate in a setting that made each audience member seem special.

Even the marquee is a full city block long in the "Showplace of the Nation" that was the ultimate destination for the brightest and best current and future stars…and *The Yong Brothers.*

The day before opening night I gave the musical conductor our music for the act; the same music that four and five piece bands had been playing for us for what seemed like years; for what actually were years.

When the curtain opened I heard the familiar melody, but goose bumps traveled throughout my body and turned the opening night jitters of being on that renowned stage into magic when I experienced the arrangement that the Conductor had created for a fifty-four piece orchestra; they were playing for us; I wanted to applaud for them. They were a symphony and yet the audience was staring at us.

Or at least I imagined they were. With all of the lights I could barely make out the audience at all. For the first time it was like I was alone yet there were thousands of eyes yards in front of me watching; a live audience that was invisible.

To describe it succinctly, the absolute highlight of my career!

For three weeks, four shows a day, I was in heaven. It was "unfortunate" that I was in our "high class" dressing room with television, phones, room service, and a pampering that I had never experienced, when Walter met the Managing Director of the *Hall* who said ours was, "the best act he had ever seen."

And yes, *The Rockettes* who lived in a dormitory within the building complete with a cafeteria and medical facilities were as breath taking as they were professed to be.

I talk about this being a dream come true, yet I wonder if what happened in the middle of our engagement might have actually *been* a dream. We were approached to perform on *The Ed Sullivan Show*, "if" we thought we could find the time. Please indulge me for a moment and repeat that sentence.

In-between the four shows we would race back and forth to the television studio for rehearsals, learning the true lack of fear found in New York cab drivers. There Walter and I were, still in costume, carrying our performing table with us, and yelling at a taxi driver to hurry…both going to the TV studio and back to *Radio City* for the next performance.

As an aside I must admit that a drive in a New York taxi is far more frightening than bears, twenty story buildings, or even finding yourself being evacuated from a country engaged in war.

I daresay I could not dance (gyrate?) as well as he could, but it was an experience to be rehearsing at the same time as Elvis Presley.

In the course of a couple of short weeks I – we – had made the humongous leap to what I considered stardom, complete with the salary that both *Radio City* and *Ed Sullivan* provided.

Outside the dressing room window and steps away from the door was the magnificent Rockefeller Center Christmas tree, inside, I was opening my Christmas present on opening night – which felt like every night.

Rockefeller Center holds its own sense of irony and could not have been a more fitting locale to fulfill our next obligation.

Come the New Year not only were *The Yong Brothers* going to be showcased in *Holiday on Ice* throughout the country, but so was Astrid. There was of course one slight handicap. To date, Astrid did not know how to ice skate. So, while we were "balancing on stage mesmerized by a symphony" four times a day, Astrid was outside on the famous rink skating, and, if I am not mistaken, working harder.

I could say without any hesitation that those who left *Radio City* everyday, those who turned off their television after *The Ed Sullivan Show*, could not have possessed the same overwhelming elation – and pride – that I felt during those weeks.

A good time to thank my father:

> *"My father gave me the greatest gift anyone could give another person: He believed in me."*
>
> ~Jim Valvano~

Chapter Nine

"Wanting something is not enough. You must hunger for it. Your motivation must be absolutely compelling in order to overcome the obstacles that will invariably come your way."

~ Les Brown~

I DON'T KNOW WHICH WORKED HARDER, my brain or my body. More precisely, I don't know which *I* worked harder. I was not then (and according to my wife of over forty years, not now) familiar with the concept of being idle. As for relaxation, the aforementioned statement sums it up.

I wanted the chance for *The Yong Brothers* to capture the *Holiday on Ice* audience the way we had at *Radio City*. As such, my brain went on overdrive (no pun intended as you will later see) while my body flexed for a new, better, more exciting feat to offer the unexpected to those who thought an ice skating rink posed limited opportunities.

No one has told me how many hours (years) are spent studying for a law or medical exam, however I am sure we rivaled their efforts with preparation of our own when my current imagination led me to achieve balancing one handed on a cane while

Walter balanced one handed on my neck; this did not appear to be a straight line, it had to be.

Yet this was not enough for me. I wanted more. I wanted something even more spectacular to include in our act for *Holiday on Ice* – and to take into account the chances were rather slim that a cane would stand perfectly erect on the ice. I do not know if I can take credit for the absurd idea that came to me for, unfortunately there is no way to say it with even a modicum of modesty, but it was brilliant.

I wanted to perform this vigorous (for both mind and body) one handed balance on a cane *on top of a car*. Walter and I practiced for what could only be compared, in hours spent, to putting 100,000 miles on a vehicle.

Boring. Thus, I wanted Astrid to drive the car while we were staring down at the roof as if it were stationary.

Still boring. I wanted to perform the entire routine on ice! Astrid was going to be what you might call a showgirl with the show and it was perfect that she join in this part of our act by driving this car with her husband and brother-in-law on the roof supported only by the point of a cane around on the ice. I must say it one more time, ice.

Being the true American that I am, I wanted to have the support of a trusted U.S. manufacturer behind me as we performed this feat. Capitalism is not only the right of citizenship but also of hereditary. In this case, who better than a car manufacturer like *Oldsmobile*. I wanted the entire routine to be performed on an *Oldsmobile* automobile with the prestige of the corporation behind us. One has to admit that a concept such as this does sort of flourish once you have passed the citizenship test as if it was a part of the exam.

A Balanced Life

I went on to begin my contact, what later would be referred to as a frustrating somewhat insurmountable conquest, with the powers that be at *Oldsmobile*. Please remember that this was a time when you did not press seven to return to the main menu, press eight for a list of employees, press nine only to get disconnected, redial and leave a thousand voice mails wondering if they had landed in a black hole. This was a time when you spoke with so many receptionists and secretaries that you could have been invited to their office party.

Astonishingly (to some, not to me) I managed not only to make my way through the corporate ladder but to even reach the President, John DeLorean.

It was my goal to showcase our act atop a *muscle car* that had never been designed (or touted by *Motor Trend*) for such usage. *Oldsmobile* loved the concept (exposure) however they wanted to unveil (feature, promote) their new *Vega*, their answer to the *Ford Pinto* and the *AMC Gremlin*, with our spectacle rather than a *muscle car*.

As for the result...

The Southern Illinoisan, Margaret Ann Nicely –

> "Holiday on Ice is having its 25th birthday, but the audiences are getting the presents...The Yong Brothers, whose acrobatics atop a moving automobile are so agile and look so impossible that one hardly notices "this little car that does everything well." Sorry about that General Motors, but Vega got upstaged."

And...

The Columbus Enquirer, Donna Wilson –

> "Holiday Balancing Act Adds Dimension to Show" – The Yong Brothers, experts in the act of balancing, performance

consists of spine-tingling balancing feats on a platform atop an automobile which moves around the ice rink as they perform and Johnny's wife, Astrid, is driving..."

"...two of the most unusual acrobats in the amusement world, the Yongs have starred in circuses, night clubs, and television..."

"...One of the most spine-tingling stunts that the Yongs perform is when Johnny balances on a steel cane with one hand, and then Walter balances with one hand on his brother's neck. It took them four years to perfect this particular act and they consider it "the most difficult and skillful one we do..."

"...a sight and family not to be missed."

We travelled with *Holiday on Ice* on a tour schedule that easily rivaled *Ringling's*; our motor home part of a caravan of our new friends, a new family of entertainers.

There was one "personal problem" that confronted me when I began with *Holiday on Ice*.

I have lived my life by not merely overcoming obstacles, but by taking the opportunity – the challenge – to transfer each obstacle into a personal accomplishment. And like most of my accomplishments, I like them to be rather *grandiose* (although others might prefer the term irrational) in nature.

The most absurd obstacle for me to even consider is that of being faced with a situation where I look foolish – not of my own accord that is.

As a young boy growing up in Germany, while others were out skating on one of the many ponds and lakes that surrounded my hometown, I was practicing. In the many locales I have travelled through from Switzerland to New York, again, while others were out skating on frozen playgrounds, when I was not performing, I was practicing. And I would be remiss to leave out that I did prefer the beaches of Sarasota to frigid, slippery, ankle twisting ideas of fun – for some. From a practical nature, my life was my body; one bad fall on the ice and I could have missed an entire season. (No, falling off the ledges of buildings or balancing on a moving vehicle does not count as risks.)

Ergo, while my brother and I performed our act to loud applause on top of a car that Astrid drove along the ice (to those in Sarasota it might seem preposterous that my wife could control a vehicle on ice when they have trouble steering through a vicious thirty mile an hour dried pavement…with their blinkers always on) what I was faced with at the end of each night's show was the obstacle that I refused to give in to.

For the finale the entire cast – me included – came skating out from backstage with the flourish of a circus' opening night; all waving and smiling as the crowds cheered and we smoothly sailed across the ice…for some.

Thus came my obstacle. After balancing one handed on a moving vehicle I now looked like a toddler taking his first steps when I "sailed" along with the rest. Remember, I did not – do not – accept obstacles where I looked like a fool – especially after the shock and praise of our act.

They will never admit it, and I cannot say for certain that it was them laughing, but I think both Walter and my wife got some sort of enjoyment watching me grab onto (some would prefer the phrase slam into) the guardrail (and it was not my fault the lights were in front of them) as I attempted to stop at the end of our *gracious* finale parade.

To put it bluntly, this was not acceptable. I cannot say for certain that I had this miraculous idea or some sort of subconscious knowledge (or innate desire to shine) but I came up with a concept to end the laughter…from *those admitting* laughter.

I took two of the small wooden blocks that I used to balance upon for handstands while Walter was either perched atop my neck or feet, and carved ruts into them. I then went on to secure ice skating blades inside the ruts. (Yes, you know where I am going with this.)

On the next evening's finale I came soaring out from backstage skating around the rink with the entire cast --- on my hands, with Walter right behind me doing the same thing. The laughter from before, and the sore ankles, was now replaced by shouts from the crowd and the admiration of the cast. I will admit that stopping still possessed problems for me.

I have no explanation for this, but feel I must share it; I have no idea how I was able to so easily skate on my hands as opposed to my feet; then again, skating is all about balance, and balance seems easier when you look at the world differently than most.

So, when faced with an obstacle, stand on your hands and the smirks turn to smiles and an obstacle into a spectacle.

In the beginning of June Astrid was forced to leave the show and return to Sarasota. Please hold back the tears, unless they are ones of joy. She was seven months pregnant and there comes a time that no matter how much of a professional you are, skating around on the ice is just not practical.

With her departure things changed drastically. All performers in our line of entertainment have a goal to obtain a long term contract at some point in their life. A period where they spend two, three years or longer under contact with a specific company or institution, be it a hotel in Las Vegas or a tour such as *Holiday on Ice*.

When the show was sold only days after Astrid's departure we were informed by the new management that our option for contractual entrainment was not to be invoked. This could be a good place to unleash those tears from before.

And just as quickly, the tears should be stopped, as it was now time to replace my ice skates with sneakers.

> *"Great works are performed not by strength but by perseverance."*
>
> ~Samuel Johnson~

Chapter Ten

*"Courage is reckoned the greatest of all virtues;
because, unless a man has that virtue,
he has no security for preserving any other."*

~ Samuel Johnson~

As opposed to many acts that perform within a circus, being hand-to-hand acrobats constantly opened new, unthought-of venues for us to showcase our talents. It is natural for an act such as ours to transgress through the circus, fairs, cabarets, night clubs, and casinos, but when I was contacted by our European agent to be a part of the *Harlem Globetrotters* "spectacle", for I am not sure what word would be appropriate, I must admit I was somewhat stunned.

I had heard of their talent before, but I had never put the connection between sports and entertainment together, until I saw their show and realized they were some of the most talented "circus performers" I had ever seen; ones that knew how to take advantage of a different setting and a different audience to achieve the same smiles and gasps from an audience that we, and all involved in the circus, had.

In truth, while the credit for talent rests completely on the *Globetrotters* themselves, their abilities might never have been realized except for their founder and creator Alan Saperstein and his successor George Gillette; two visionaries that had the ability to see how creative genius, if you will, could fill an unknown void in the sports arena.

And in this golden age of the *Harlem Globetrotters* came two of their most renown and gifted athletes (entertainers, showman, comics, gymnasts?), Meadowlark Lemon and Curly Neil.

I really don't have any other way of putting this, but it was fun being on the court with them, and I never thought I would say the word court and me in the same sentence, then again, I didn't know years ago I was a "winning bodybuilder" either – I guess there is a cross over between acrobatic art and sports that I had never really considered; and the *Globetrotters* were definite proof. I watched their "act" with broad smiles and truly learned from the way they manipulated the smiles and cheers from the audience.

In Europe *The Yong Brothers* toured with the *Globetrotters* through almost every major city: Paris, London, Vienna to mention but a few. However, our first evening in Amsterdam could have put a halt to my debut and entire experience in a sporting arena.

After *openings nacht* my brother and I loaded the bus with the entire "acrobatic" entourage. There was an unspoken rule of travel with the *Harlem Globetrotters* which all failed to tell us. Which is the most absurd concept; unspoken, yet we were supposed to know.

All of the performers in the show, from the "rival" team that played "against" the *Globetrotters* every night to the intermission exhibitionists such as ourselves, were "supposed" to sit in the back of the bus while the *Globetrotters* sat in the front. I choose not to go into the psychological or political meaning behind this.

Unknowingly Walter and I took seats near the front of the bus and no one, including Meadowlark Lemon who was sitting near us, gave us any indication that we should vacate our seats and move "to the back of the bus." We waited quite a while for one last *Globetrotter* to join us and when he staggered onto the bus beer in hand, and looking like a "seasoned contortionist" as he bent his body to move through the aisle, he stopped right in front of me. Leaning over (as if he had a choice) he told us, in words I prefer not to print, "To get to the back of the bus."

I was ready to confront him right then, and when Walter noticed, I gave him a look that he quickly understood to mean don't stop me or you're the one who will regret it. I got up and, ironically, I was standing face to face with the blowhard since he was bent over in the bus - if we had been in any locale where he could stand erect I would have been looking into his chest - and, in no uncertain terms, told him, "Who the hell are you to tell me where to sit? (Possibly said more emphatically)"

As some of the players pushed him into another seat he (foaming at the mouth) told me he would take care of me outside the hotel tonight! This literal giant of a man wanted to beat the #$$@$% out of me for sitting in a seat, not "his seat", "a" seat. I don't care if he was nine feet tall, I was not, never have been, never would be, one to back down to some thug who threatened me.

Before I could even tie my own shoelaces I had been travelling from town to town, always faced with young hooligans who wanted to taunt the new kid, the different kid, the one in the circus. There were times when I was antagonized by gypsy children who traveled with the circus, out of fear, bullying, or protection of their home turf I had no idea, but they were part of my reality. I never once backed down to them. It was not something I was taught and I cannot even describe it as innate, but I knew that if I started my life being pushed around, then I always would be.

When I got older, and still traveling to places where I didn't know which parts of town to stay clear of, and also worked alongside the roust abouts who in truth were nothing more than sketchy, rowdy men doing anything for a buck, I learned the (their) seedier side of life. In the circus this was further complicated by unexplainable phenomena that in certain cities "gangs of brawlers" would come to the circus encampment to make fun of, taunt, and want to kick the crap out of the "freak circus people."

As my career progressed, there were instances in casinos or cabarets where I encountered unruly drunks or, for lack of a better term, low lifes, who always wanted to cause a scene with me or someone close to me.

In all cases I defended myself. I did not go looking for physical confrontation, but I did not back down. It was not an option.

Growing up the way I did, learning to survive and protect myself when necessary amid certain elements and mentalities, I learned "tricks of the trade" from those I was forced to encounter. Regardless of size, there is an art to being (surviving, winning) in a brawl that can only be learned from the kind of people who I occasionally came into contact with.

The behemoth who threatened me on the bus was a challenge. Not one I wanted to deal with, one I had to find a way to deal with.

Outside of the hotel, alone in the rain, I waited for the "monster" who wanted to teach me a #$$%# lesson. I was pumped with adrenaline (and fear as any intelligent indivudal should be) while I waited. But I came prepared. Prepared to defend myself.

I was clutching a roll of quarters in each of my hands; I had learned from people who lived on the street the tricks they used; I knew the force; I knew what it could stop. "Stop" is the key word.

I waited until I was soaked -- and he never appeared.

The next day I met Meadowlark Lemon who confided in me that he had told the guy who couldn't wait to beat me to the ground that I, the man at least six inches and seventy pounds lighter than him, would have left him bleeding. Ergo, the "tower with a mouth" never showed up that night. I can't say with certainty what would have happened had he shown, I can say that winning without fighting is the best scenario.

It was only one day later that George Gillette called the brainless Neanderthal back to the States; it was not long after that that he was forced to find another job.

And the *Harlem Globetrotters*? They called me Strongman!

Funny, that name brought back a memory of my mother when I was just a teen. She told me how strong I was and that I needed to watch myself to make sure I never hurt anyone, that I didn't know my own strength. Are mothers always right?

Before I set you astray, let me assure you that the next two months touring with the *Globetrotters* was truly remarkable.

From this unconventional venue of entertainment, in June we went on to Portugal where we performed with an elaborate floor show at the *Estoril Hotel*, unfortunately I had to "put up with" being near *The Bluebell Girls* again!

As an aside, it is said that the *Estoril* was the inspiration, possible setting, for Ian Fleming's *Casino Roayle*. If you saw the interior and the patrons you would understand why. It appalls me that if you walk into a Vegas casino today you see people in shorts and jeans, it astonishes me that even when I was on stage there back in the sixties it seemed like an evening jacket was reserved for the performers while the guests "sometimes" acquiesced to a tie. There is a level of class that never seemed to make the trans-Atlantic voyage.

I do not know whether you would call it another case of yin and yang or a spiritual statement, but after only four weeks at the *Estoril* an event occurred to manifest the aforementioned regardless of which definition you prefer.

I received a telegram that my son, Tyrone, was born. An hour later I received a second telegram, that my father had passed away…an hour after my son was born…in the same hospital. With the joy of being a father again, and the sadness of losing a father, Walter and I next went to the *Casino Travemünde* in Germany, a nightclub that truly rivaled *The Lido*, but the best was yet to come.

The most famous nightclub on Italy's Amalfi Coast is the *Africana Club*. It is a club hidden by secular rocks and set deep within the rock face with a winding staircase in a magnificent underground cave full of illuminated stalagmites and, for patrons as opposed to employees, reached by the sea. And the international entertainment truly parallels the spectacular setting.

Without going into details, let me allude to the premise that the *Club* was frequented by a wealthy clientele one might "expect" in southern Italy, and managed by the same aforementioned society with both precision and elegance.

On stage one evening I was in the process of rising myself into a handstand and getting ready to balance on my head as a "patron" of the club made a loud noise heckling me. I proceeded on with the feat as my brother balanced on top of me and did my best to ignore the jeering from the heckler and concentrated on my routine. If I was angry at the time, it compared nothing to the anger I had toward that "man" when the act was finished.

A Balanced Life

I went from backstage to confront the scum only to find that he was no longer at his table; the waiters had taken it upon themselves to "escort" the man out of the club and after that, well, I can only speculate…and hope.

In all sincerity, words cannot due justice to the imaginative, glorious environment of the *Africana Club*.

The end of 1971 brought me back to what was fast becoming a tradition as I found myself celebrating the holiday with my family on the beach in Sarasota; what a horrible way to spend a winter.

Yet I shouldn't say a winter as much as couple of months, for before long we were once again up and touring with the *Harlem Globetrotters* throughout the United States. A special engagement for me as my wife would be performing as well; no doubt one of the shorter people on the basketball court.

The schedule the *Globetrotters* kept made the *Ringling* schedule look like prolonged engagements; one city, one night. To keep this monumental pace the *Globetrotters* traveled in a refurbished elegant bus – a combination of a limousine and a coach – while me, my family, and my brother rode behind them in our motor homes loaded with our equipment.

On one occasion this was not feasible as they had to perform one day in Chicago and the next in Los Angeles. They were flying and it was impossible for us to fly with all of our equipment; it was way beyond conceivable that we could drive there that fast – even for me. As such they went on alone and we were going to drive and meet them in San Francisco for the next booking…two days away.

As the 1972 season came to a close I took stock of my limited sports knowledge realizing that while basketball teams might play home for a few days, take a few days off, and then proceed to another city, the *Globetrotters* were far from a sports team. They had

Johnny Yong

the agility of athletes and the stage presence of showmen…with the schedule of a circus.

Call me foolish, but while as wonderful as the tour had been, I decided that I prefer a theater to a basketball court.

A Balanced Life

Chapter Eleven

*"Our greatest glory is not in never failing,
but in getting up every time we do."*

~ Confucius~

JUST PRIOR TO THE END OF MY "CAREER ON THE COURT," I received a call from the *Circus Circus* in Las Vegas which was interested in having us perform and, if we would like the opportunity, we would need to <u>audition</u> in person prior to a commitment. As opposed to sounding egotistical, I report the reaction of the performers who knew *The Yong Brothers* act when they said, "they were literally shocked (although circus people tend to use more colorful language) that we would need to audition."

Ego aside, it took no thought whatsoever for us to audition. As with *Holiday on Ice*, and even more so as this was a stationary venue, we were determined to find employment that was secure, a contract of length rather than the sporadic life that any entertainer encounters. In essence, the uncertainty of what the next job would be; where the next paycheck was coming from. No matter how wonderful it was to receive a large fee for a "two week engagement", there was nothing like the peace of mind of weekly payroll – especially from Las Vegas.

The audition was a non-disputable requirement as the owner Jay Sarno, who had conceived *Caesars's Palace*, his other icon on the Las Vegas Strip, insisted on reviewing and hiring the acts in *his* hotel.

Circus Circus was his dream to create a house that harbored the largest permanent big top in the world.

Like a big top, the huge casino had numerous circus acts performing around the cavernous room, trapeze and high wire acts performing over the heads of gamblers and bevies of showgirls dancing and singing throughout the casino as well as in each of the 14 bars and restaurants in the building.

While other Las Vegas casinos had catered to adults with children in minor ways, Jay Sarno's *Circus Circus* was regarded as the first to market directly to family vacationers, complete with the only RV Park on the strip, although he also sought big spending gamblers

To keep the kids away from the casino, Sarno built a circular midway on the second floor, overlooking the casino, with carnival-type games and space to watch the circus performers.

While Jay Sarno gave the final approval to our employment, we were in effect hired by Pete Cristiani who came from an elite family of circus performers who, with his family, had performed with *Ringling Bros. and Barnum & Bailey*, *Hagenbeck-Wallace*, *L.G. Barnes*, *Floyd King* and other circuses, and went from performer to management.

Not only was *The Yong Brothers* given a one year contract with a one year option, Astrid was also hired to astound the audience with her act that had been delighting spectators throughout the

A Balanced Life

world. 1973, the entire family on stage at the *Circus Circus*!

This was, for lack of a better (although there can not be a more demonstrative) phrase, "The Frank Sinatra" era of Vegas; a time when you were required to be in jacket and tie in the casino, and if you didn't have one, the casino would happily *rent* you one. Simply put, the class and ambience that was meant to be, not what it has become.

Although I cannot say (even if some might) that I possess the same magnetism as Sean Connery or Roger Moore, but there was some sort of *aura* following me. When I had performed in Portugal at the *Estoril* it was said to have been the setting and inspiration for Ian Fleming's *Casino Royale*. *Circus Circus'* famous midway was featured in the film *Diamonds Are Forever*. I might not have been able to follow in either of the two aforementioned stars' footsteps, but I doubt they could follow in my handprints!

Circus Circus itself could only really be described as an all encompassing experience to all who entered its doors. In his typical and rather unusual flair, in his journalistic novel of the early '70s, *Fear and Loathing in Las Vegas*, Hunter S. Thompson wrote, *"The Circus-Circus is what the whole hep world would be doing Saturday night if the Nazis had won the war. This is the sixth Reich. The ground floor is full of gambling tables, like all the other casinos . . . but the place is about four stories high, in the style of a circus tent, and all manner of strange County-Fair/Polish Carnival madness is going on up in this space."*

In-between shows, which were four times a day, I would some times help Astrid with her routine by either bringing props to her on stage or acting as her *showman*, and at other times I would *force* myself to gamble…for a *short break* awaiting my next performance.

When I arrived in Vegas I had no intention on gambling at all. I used to play cards while I was in the army, but when you have played as many casinos as I have, and are spending your days full time performing in one for an extended period of time, the last thing I wanted to do is start gambling away what I worked so hard to earn.

In Las Vegas this proves entirely too difficult. You can go into a grocery store or a gas station and you are faced with the *one armed bandits* (of which I had no desire or temptation to challenge) and in my life virtually every daily activity from going to get my mail or to reach my dressing room led me through the casino.

As such, I occasionally played Keno, stayed away (if I didn't I was being possessed, it was not me standing there throwing dice) from the craps table (which I loved to play), but somehow *convinced* myself to play cards…for fun (isn't that what everyone says?)

Who would have thought that it would be sitting at a card table as opposed to being up on stage that would make me a Las Vegas *icon*.

I was sitting with a group of five people and with each new shuffle of the cards the dealer would pass the deck to the next player in line to cut the cards; when it was passed to me I merely tapped the top of the deck indicating that I had no need to actually cut the deck. For no apparent reason the person playing next to me gave me what could best be considered a "growl."

As we all continued to play the "growling person" next to me was losing, not in the best of spirits (to put it mildly), and like other losers, cursing his luck as well as *me* for not having the *intelligence* to cut the cards.

A Balanced Life

Once again the dealer passed the deck to me for my turn to cut the cards and again I simply tapped the top of the deck. The individual next to me started yelling at me, telling me I had to cut the cards, what was wrong with me, I had to cut the cards – over and over again until I just lost it with this arrogant $$#%$%.

I grabbed the deck, told him if he wanted me to cut the $$#%$ deck then fine I would. With that I took hold of the entire deck with both hands, ripped the entire stack in half, through them on the table, and said, "Here, I cut your $$#%$ cards!"

Let me be clear. I had never done anything like this before. I never knew I could do it. Once again, I guess my mother was right.

In that one moment I became the new "sideshow" of Vegas, although I prefer the term "talk of the town." Everywhere I went people seemed to have heard about my "feat" and wanted to see me do it again. People would literally come to the *Circus Circus* just to see me "cut the cards."

I should mention that Mr. Sarno never offered me a commission for this *act* that brought patrons to the hotel explicitly for this reason and then, well, of course they might as well gamble for a while as long as they were there.

I haven't *cut* a deck of cards in half with my bare hands for many years and I can offer no logical progression for what ensued, but somehow a few years after the Vegas "event" I found myself tearing entire phone books in half whenever the story of the cards emerged.

Recently, at the *young age of seventy-five*, I was telling this story to someone while he looked at with me with a combination of awe and disbelief – with heavy emphasis on the latter - until I grabbed a yellow page directory from the counter and tore it in half.

I can say with *one hundred percent* accuracy that he is still very much in awe without a shred of disbelief!

Really, I was just playing cards to see if I could win some money – excuse me, have some fun - before my next show.

In November of 1973, at the end of our first year, our option was not picked up for a further twelve moths. It was the *judgment* of management that the heightened interest in circus acts had enabled them to get two acts to perform for the price they were paying one.

With the disposable of Astrid's equipment far out in the desert marking the end of her career, it was once again time to begin looking for work.

My disappointment of not having a more permanent stay with *Circus Circus* is only further fueled when today I see performers who I knew and performed with back in 1968 when they really were destitute; arriving at a stage door with cardboard boxes as their suitcases, and clothes that probably deserved to be carried by such luggage, on their way to a career that had little chance of prospering. Through the aid of *The Lido* they did manage to escalate their career *slightly* better than card board boxes and get *somewhat* of a permanent following in Vegas. Ironic, they also happened to have been born in my area of Germany.

The names of these once destitute performers who I worked with over forty years ago and now have gained a *little bit* of respect in Vegas: *Siegfried and Roy*

> 'The distance between insanity and genius is measured only by success"
>
> ~Ian Fleming~

A Balanced Life

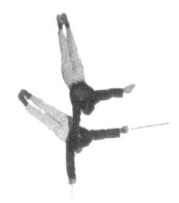

Chapter Twelve

*"Courage is resistance to fear, mastery of fear,
not absence of fear."*

~ Mark Twain~

AFTER TWO MONTHS OF TRYING TO FIND ENGAGEMENTS in Vegas we were contacted by Switzerland's *Circus Knie*, who I had the privilege of working with "all those years ago" in 1951, stored our mobile homes at a friend's house, and looked forward to our return to Europe.

In March of 1974, travelling from city to city throughout Switzerland, it was as if a new era of my career (or what you might call a return to) was beginning as we once again became European stars. Possibly a bit embellished, but I report from what the papers proclaimed, not my own ego.

Circus Knie had heard about a creation, an invention if you will, that we devised (although did not have time to implement) in Vegas that they wanted featured in their circus; something spectacular – from their point of view, mine…and the audience.

A rotating platform with me doing a free headstand on a small pole with Walter extended in a handstand balancing on my feet – but that was merely the beginning. The "pole" I was balancing on was actually a "telescope" that began to rise, and rise, and rise, until it soared twenty-two feet in the air with me still on my head and Walter balancing above me. A three foot platform, twenty-two feet of telescopic extension, my five foot-six inch body combined with Walter's extended balance from "standing" atop my feet on his hands adding seven feet to the extension…all had us balancing – on my head – almost thirty-eight feet above the stage with Walter's toes touching the aerialist's wire…with a platform rotating!

It might have not previewed in Vegas, but Switzerland and *Circus Knie's* audience were going to be the first to marvel at "my" creation and our hours of practice and dedication to providing thrills to all who attended.

The feat itself was a success, but not on our opening night in Rapperswil in front of patrons. The entire apparatus had been built for a stage (i.e. Vegas) where the castors on the platform could roll the heavy machinery into view. The circus (i.e. *Knie*) was not performed on a stage but on what could only be described as a soft earth. It was impossible to roll the equipment out; it was virtually impossible to lift it until we actually had to have six stage hands carry it out like a litter. The disappoint and frustration of this opening night fiasco down played the unveiling of the act itself. Eventually a duel trolley system was created that enabled us to roll the equipment out, albeit slowly, and we were able to gain the *astonishment and thunderous applause of the audience*. Or as Rapperswil's newspaper DIE LINTH can be quoted, "FANTASTISCH!!!"

That was until the next city.

In St. Gallen I was excited beyond belief to perform our "40' spectacle" for the audience as it rolled on stage. That lasted for approximately thirty seconds when it was plugged into an electrical outlet and blacked out close to half of the city! The director had reached his frustration level. He decided to cut the phenomena from the show. I can not say assuredly whether it was the disappoint over the cancellation, or the hurt to my pride for I had created the act that tested our commitment and talent, that unnerved me the most.

That was until the famous *Bronley*, renowned for his space rocket that opened above the audience for him to perform aerial acts on, entered the picture. He had a hobby, if you ask me a master at, of building electronic gadgets and said he could fix it. We had been using a voltage converter box; he managed to rewire the entire mechanism to the proper voltage.

The obstacle of weight had been conquered. Electricity was no longer a problem. The entire season was a success, or as DIE TAT had reviewed in Bern, Zurich, and Geneva: "FANTASTIQUE!"

As for Geneva, I will have to say that the praise I received directly from Charlie Chaplin and Princess Grace of Monaco one evening was far more dramatic and endearing than the words of the press.

When the season with *Knie* came to a close, in November of 1974 we went to Scotland for a holiday season at *Kelvin Hall*, a venue with an indoor circus, rides, and overall carnival atmosphere.

Our reception in Scotland treated me (us) as if in fact (okay, I'm exaggerating) I was 007, Sean Connery:

THE WORLD'S FAIR – Fraser Dudgeon – "...*Happy BALANCE of acts at Kelvin Hall...the animals don't steal the show. I was delighted again to see the superb act of the two Yong Brothers whom I last saw in Copenhagen in 1950.*

Among the tricks displayed were a handstand on the feet of the bearer who was in a free headstand. Later the bearer assumed the same position and the top mounter performed a headstand on his feet. There was a handstand on the neck of the bearer who was also in a handstand position, then came a single handstand on a hand rod by the bearer with the top man also performing a single handstand on his neck.

However, the best trick for in my opinion was the bearer in a fully extended hand stand position with the top man duplicating on the bearer's feet and then the bearer walking on his hands.

An act to be seen again and again and savored completely!"

Almost unheard of for a director, especially during the Christmas season, was that he allowed us to leave the show for two days to appear in Monaco (my first experience but far from my last) for the *Festival International Du Cirque Monte Carlo*. After a two day thrill, and once again the chance to perform on the same bill as my friend the incomparable *Charlie Rivel*, we returned to Scotland to finish out the Holiday season.

I would say you could take a breath now, but unfortunately there is no time for we immediately went to Copenhagen to join *Circus Benneweis* for the 1975 season. Not only am I happy to say that our telescopic balance apparatus and routine worked wonderfully, but we made it through the entire season without a single water tower exploding!

I imagine there was still room for one more stamp on my passport, for the 1976 season was spent traveling throughout Germany with *Circus Barum*.

October 1976 we returned to Sarasota for a long extended stay back in the United States. *One month.*

A Balanced Life

With Astrid in Sarasota, Walter and I flew to Las Vegas to retrieve our motor homes that we had stored at a friend's house and drive them across country to New Jersey in order to ship them to Europe for our next tour. Cargo being transported across the Atlantic is charged by bulk. Two motor homes, need I say more?

After our four weeks of *relaxing* in America we flew to Le Havre, France to await the delivery of our motor homes; a journey that should have taken four weeks. It was November, apparently the worst season for cross-Atlantic travel and the shipment took an extra week. While this might not sound overly traumatic, we had a Christmas engagement at the *Circus Medrano* in Naples and lest I remind you, "No Play – No Pay."

The motor homes arrived and thus began our mad dash through Europe. The gas tanks had been virtually emptied for the journey, so we drove a few miles to the nearest gas station and completely filled our tanks. I am fluent in French. I should have known better. I filled the tanks with diesel! Less than thirty feet from the gas station white smoke came bellowing out of the exhaust pipe and the engine was louder than a twelve piece orchestra.

We remedied this fiasco (do you know how much it costs to fill up the gas tank of a motor home?) and I can say with one hundred percent honesty, this was the *only easy part* of our journey through Switzerland to southern Italy.

When we arrived in Brig, at the base of the Alps, we were afraid that Walter's motor home would not be able to make it through the tunnel (his being higher than mine) and were forced to drive the *Simplon Pass* over the Alps, securing each tire with chains to facilitate the snow.

Please forget the motor home for a brief moment and just take into account the Swiss Alps – winter. As I drove up the mountain

I was lucky that I was not claustrophobic as eighteen foot walls of snow and ice clutched each side of the vehicle on the one lane road; that is one *single* lane used for *both* directions. The motor home was no more than a luge encased in its tunnel. In the lowest gear possible I finally made it to the top of the mountain not knowing what was awaiting me on what was now the Italian side of the Alps.

The road was *no* where near as cleared and drivable as the Swiss side; yet you are at the top, what can you do?

The motor home was in its lowest gear and all of a sudden I could feel it…the breaks wouldn't hold…I was slipping on the ice…sliding on ice thousands of feet above sea level on a mountain road with no guard rails. As I was sliding around a curve it was not the breaks that caused me to begin my conversation with God, but the fact that the trailer I was pulling behind me jack-knifed. One lane of ice and snow. A jack-knifed vehicle. My wife and daughter behind me facing God knows what as she followed in our car, and Walter following behind her – all of us screeching around turns in the clouds and as I was clutching my son in my arms ready to jump from the vehicle and let it plummet through the sky.

In an instant, it happened. It was out of my control.

It just happened.

The tires gripped. We began to slow on our final descent into Domodossola. Most people pull into a rest stop and race to the bathroom. This was not a necessity for me.

At that moment, the thought of venturing back onto the road was far from my mind. Do I need to mention "No Play – No Pay" again? Back on our journey south it was snowing continuously, but that seemed like a dream compared to the nightmare only minutes before.

We arrived in Florence with the snow apparently behind us

and there was no choice but to rest for the night, to relax…to take a deep breath. Astrid wanted to keep going to avoid the snow. I quickly informed her that *it does not snow in Florence*. Possibly not for most, but on this journey I was "unsurprisingly" wrong.

I awoke in the middle of the night and looked out the window to find the entire rest area – us included - had been covered in a snow storm. Trying to open up the door I found out that we were sealed in as the heater on top of the home had melted the snow and ice formed on the door. Yet this was *not* the worst of the situation.

I turned and heard it. What a husband dreads most. *"So, it doesn't snow in Florence?!"* After all that I had been through I did the only thing a man in my position could do, I started to uncontrollably laugh – *with* my wife.

Then came the only other natural course of action. I turned on the engine and just plowed right out of there with the other vehicles following me.

Arriving in Naples, just on time for opening, the Director was confident that we had decided to make money on the side by taking brief Christmas bookings on our journey south, thus explaining our late arrival.

He didn't need to call witnesses in Domodossola to validate our journey. He saw the truth on my face.

Christmas 1976 with the *Circus Medrano* in Naples; I know why *Ringling* spent the winter in Sarasota.

> *"There is much in the world to make us afraid.*
> *There is much more in our faith to make us unafraid."*
>
> ~Frederick W. Cropp~

Chapter Thirteen

*"Whatever I have tried to do in life,
I have tried with all my heart to do it well;
whatever I have devoted myself to,
I have devoted myself to completely."*

~Charles Dickens~

BY MARCH OF 1977 MOST OF THE SHAKING IN MY BODY from our journey over the Alps only a few months ago had dissipated from my hands (please note than when you spend your life viewing the world "upside down" trembling of the hands is tantamount to a football player with a limp) and we began our tour with France's *Circus AMAR*.

AMAR was produced by Firmin Bouglione, whose name was as synonymous with the Circus in France as Ringling's was in America, and continually brought the thoughts of traveling – being - with my family twenty-five years ago back to life. All the memories were within me, yet at times it is almost as if I was viewing someone else's life from eons, rather than years, ago.

Bouglione's *AMAR* possessed all of the recollections that many hold of their earliest, magical, visits to the circus – the birthdays and holiday treats - from the red and white tents with flapping flags to semis afire with the circus logo as they traveled into your town announcing the arrival of the circus as you greeted them with smiles *almost* as large as the happiest clown.

In keeping with Bouglione tradition of excellence, not only did *AMAR* feature *The Yong Brothers* but starred the incomparable and indescribable *Zavatta*.

Unlike the trip venturing through France and Switzerland what seemed like only days (or at times decades) ago, in this case the motor home was a blessing - aside from the fact that I acted as my own mechanic, plumber, and electrician. It was a place to call home and as we travelled with the family from place to place the kids would study with Astrid (*adding* to the invaluable knowledge that is not found in books when in each new city they found themselves in new cultures grasping foreign languages with the dexterity that only a child can) and had the opportunity to play around the Winnebago while one of us watched them that would never have been possible in the nomadic bustle of hotels and transient beds.

While I wouldn't be as bold to say we did it *solely* for educational value, it was fabulous to sightsee as we followed the circus route stopping at vineyards and sites what Americans would call ancient history but the French would say, "Please, it's only a couple of hundred years old." Or more appropriately, *"Ce n'est que s'il vous plaît quelques cent ans vieux."*

As we travelled in our large Winnebago with our American license plates the locales had no idea that we were circus performers en route to our next location, but thought of as *les Américains riches.*

At the end of the season, and after a brief period of exploration

A Balanced Life

for the kids (rest for me) in February of 1978 we were set to begin our engagement at the *Cabaret de Monte Carlo* located within the glamorous and stately *Casino de Monte Carlo*; an environment that had an almost forgotten mandate in *other* places: *Correct Attire Mandatory At All Times.*

We found a beautiful place to park along the hills of Monaco and although I did not see (accept?) the cloud covering that was descending upon me, Astrid insisted that Tyrone, now seven, was having more and more problems walking and he needed to see a doctor.

At Prince Rainer's insistence (more appropriately phrased, "hospitality") we took Tyrone to his private doctor, Dr. Alan Frere.

The audience is quiet as the man slowly lowers himself into the cannon, the band plays a slight drum roll, the fuse on the cannon is ignited as the audience gapes waiting for what is about to come, when a loud explosion echoes through the arena as a man soars into the air and lands hundreds of feet away in a net smiling and waving to the crowd.

The circus.

Parents sit beside their child in a doctor's office, the flame has already ignited the fuse, the drum roll is louder in their heads than anything ever heard within the big top as they await for the doctor to let the cannon explode and soar the man – the boy – into the net hundreds of feet away.

Only this time there is no net, no applause.

Life.

When the doctor lets the words come out of his mouth it was the loudest explosion I had ever heard. Tyrone, my son, had Muscular Dystrophy.

The following day we took him to the children's hospital in

Nice and after hearing my boy cry out in pain as they infused long needles into his legs for a muscular biopsy the doctor confirmed the diagnosis: muscular dystrophy.

I felt helpless, I felt devastated, I felt…

That night I had to go on stage and make an audience of young and old alike smile and applaud while I was empty inside except knowing that I had no choice but to be on the stage that evening.

Before I was old enough to stop looking under my bed at night for the bogey man I knew what it was like to go without food, what it meant to struggle albeit how hard my parents worked to undermine the state of our lives. I was born in a period of extreme hardship that I am not able to narrate, yet more importantly I learned what it meant to survive, how to cope with whatever reality threw in front of me and continue on knowing that if I had overcome one obstacle I could conquer them all; a mentality that assuredly seems idealistic; realistically (at least to me), necessary - and invaluable - without a doubt.

The world had been my teacher and I had learned what survival meant and part of that survival was also learning the value of commitment, not just to myself but to the people who hired me, to those I performed for.

Could I limit myself to say that if I did not go on stage at *Radio City* due to illness I wouldn't have been paid - no play, no pay? No. I made a commitment to myself to be there that night because I had made a commitment to the management, and more importantly to those in the audience who came to se me perform…to smile and escape to the circus (theater) for the evening.

I *went* on - be it stage - or life - I *go* on - survival. So the night after the visit to the hospital, the confirmation of my son's fate, I went on that stage…or at least my body did. I cannot say if the audience applauded, for as the moment I finished the last segment of the act, they were oblivious to me.

As we were preparing to leave Monte Carlo I managed to reach Jerry Lewis whom I had met while in Vegas when he was already doing his amazing work to educate and find a cure for Muscular Dystrophy – a disease with no cure, with only one outcome – and he was kind enough to refer me to a specialist in England, so yes, I still had hope for what was considered hopeless.

In April we arrived in Blackpool England and began our year long tour with the *Black Tower Circus*. Since I am not a firm believer in coincidence, what I found in Blackpool was almost too absurd to comprehend as my life seemed to be part of a cinema saga: they had just finished filming parts of James Bond's latest adventure *The Spy Who Loved Me*. By this point I contemplated drinking martinis, *shaken* of course.

The *buzz* about our act high above the stage had travelled to England, however here I stupidly agreed to perform the trick under dire circumstances. I (we) was atop a platform that was surrounded by water where fountains would emerge as we elevated toward the ceiling. The fountains were far from sublime to me and Walter as the water spewed from actual *stakes* around the platform that I was *head balanced* on. In hindsight I can say, "Would James Bond have done that?" or for that matter, "*Could* James Bond have done that?"

I set up residence with the Winnebago a few miles from the hectic seaside boardwalk where *Black Tower Circus* performed in a locale that we were able to make into a home, a happy place for us and the children. In an effort to truly enjoy my neighborhood environment I planted a vegetable garden complete with onions, parley, chives, and cabbage. Important? Of course! I worked hard at those vegetables and I was proud of them.

I awoke one morning hearing noise from outside the front door. My vegetable garden, the garden that I had put so much love and time into (okay, I'm sounding a bit dramatic) was not only being trampled upon by a horse but the nag was eating my vegetables! I ran outside yelling and screaming like a maniac at this *creature* that was eating *my* parsley.

I swear I punched the horse right in its long snout and knocked it out cold, but what do I know, I also thought I was drinking *shaken* martinis waiting for Moneypenny to call. The decision is yours.

In-between shows, where Astrid was helping with our act, she took Tyrone to London to see the specialist at Hammersmith Hospital that Jerry Lewis managed to arrange for Tyrone to see.

Astrid returned with the same negative answers, the same prophetic diagnosis. And life continued.

In 1979 we joined Italy's *Circus Medrano, Il Circo Famoso Nel Mondo*; we drove over the Alps during the spring on this occasion (where I was fortunate enough to partake of the restrooms) and performed with *Medrano* for the entire season.

At the end of the season we accepted an engagement that was more reminiscent of Lebanon than any of my travels throughout Europe. *The Yong Brothers* were asked to perform in *Persia* at Tehran's *Night Club Baccarat*.

The club, a haven for the wealthy of the country, was a grandiose casino complete with a lavish show of strippers, belly dancers, and, of course, us. Although the engagement was too good to pass up, we were *strongly* advised that due to the *political climate* of the country it would be best if Astrid and the children remained in Nice.

The *Night Club Baccarat*, like most venues we had performed in throughout Europe, retained our passports and papers while we were under contract and then would amicably return them upon our departure. In Tehran the *amicable* part seemed to have been forgotten. We were *suggested* to provide *baksheesh*, a term used to describe political corruption and bribery in the Middle East, more politically correct, "lavish remuneration and bribes, rudely demanded but ever so graciously accepted by the natives in return for little or no services rendered."

Upon our departure our passports were not only checked at airport security, but at the gate and even on the plane itself; all requiring some form of *Baksheesh*.

And the hassle we encountered along with the *graciously accepted tips* were a blessing compared to staying. Only one month later on February 11, 1979 the country went through devastating upheaval as the Shah was overthrown and Americans were evacuated – the ones that were able to.

1980 was spent independently touring throughout Italy at various discotheques, cabarets, and nightclubs and with the luxury of being booked into theaters for two week periods, it actually was a wonderful year that managed to encompass both performing and the warmth of family life.

1981 was *playtime* for (most of) the family as we performed in Germany's land of enjoyment, its most visited amusement park *Phantasialand*. If all of the visitors could enjoy this park that delighted families with roller coasters, amusements, fun-filled shows and themed "lands" of Berlin, Mexico, China, Africa and Fantasy, then why shouldn't we? Three shows a day could not interfere with living in *Das "Magische Königreichvon" Deutschland.*

Each day I tried to think of a new way to entertain, to bring enjoyment, to Tyrone. As such I picked up the hobby of electric trains. In all fairness I don't think that anything I have ever undertaken would be considered a mere hobby, more like an obsession to perfection. Thus in my "spare time" I built Tyrone an entire Alpine Village for his trains to travel through…and yes, I did let him play with it as well.

I had parked the motor home near the trailers of the *Nicolini Brothers* who, I found out while *sniffing* around their trailers, thrilled the audience with a chimpanzee act. On the first day I was aware of my new neighbors I went up to their trailer and mistakenly walked right in to confront an animal (beast?) that could have frightened the tigers and lions into their cages without a whip or chair.

A Rottweiler (elephant?) who ironically became Tyrone's *protector* on the days he was sitting in front our motor home. Forgive my lack of humor, but a Rottweiler named Bella?

Unfortunately not all of the Nicolini's *pets* treated Tyrone as well. One evening he was backstage watching me perform and as I was coming off stage I could see one of the chimps – the largest one – making its way towards Tyrone's chair the way an animal hunts its prey. In the land of the jungle, animals, when they sense one of their pride is ill, unable to keep up with the pact, kill the injured to protect the purity of the whole.

The chimp thought – *sensed* - the same of Tyrone – *only* that one time.

The entire season went very well and as it ended we were offered an engagement in Switzerland but we (I especially) were

A Balanced Life

also faced with evaluating our own reality.

Walter had decided that it was time to retire the act; time to leave the stage before the media started labeling us hacks and to go the way we wanted to be remembered – as stars.

I was *confused*.

Max Frimberger – *Captain Max Frimberger*, a close friend who I had performed with while with *Ringling*, insisted (and came very close to convincing me) that I should heed Walter's advice, not only was it time for me to retire but there was a position in the Sarasota County Sheriff's Department where he worked and he was sure I could gain employment.

I was *swayed*.

Tyrone needed a stable environment without any of the limitations, obstacles, which he faced on the road.

I was *convinced*.

October second, nineteen hundred and eighty-one was the last performance for *The Yong Brothers*.

The first time I heard the sound of those two hands meeting together, praising, in awe of what I had done on stage I was five years old – 1940.

That day the *beginning of my life* transpired at the *Wintergarten Theater* in Berlin.

The last time I heard that applause for all I was accomplishing, for all of the entertaining, for all of the pleasure I was giving the audience by balancing on my hands and my head was as at the *Wintergarten Theater* in Brühl.

As it was in 1940, the *Wintergarten* in 1981 was *another beginning*.

"*Man is made by his belief. As he believes, so he is.*"
~Johann Wolfgang von Goethe~

Chapter Fourteen

*"To accomplish great things,
we must not only act, but also dream
not only plan, but also believe."*

~ Anatole France~

AFTER TRAVELING FROM BERLIN TO NEW YORK, PARIS to Los Angeles, Copenhagen to Chicago, Madrid to Montana, London to San Diego, Korea to Lebanon (I think you get the idea) and literally clustering up every page with visa stamps in over eight passports, I had not experienced *true* culture shock.

Mastering six languages, being stopped by police in three continents, looking down the end of a rifle – from both sides - I *still* had not experienced *true* culture shock.

Performing in front of royalty and on the world's best stages from Las Vegas to Monte Carlo, once again I had not experienced *true* culture shock.

On October nineteenth, nineteen hundred and eighty-one I did; I was inducted into the Sarasota County Sheriff's Department.

People take many turns in their professional lives, often even when that professionalism defines who they are, yet going from banker to lawyer or salesman to chef pales beyond comparison to after forty years of performing with the circus, spending your life as an acrobat where more time is spent on your hands than on your feet, to becoming a law enforcement officer.

Sarasota had been the winter home for over fifty years to the circus, and as such, many entertainers (I cannot use the adjective "past" for in truth it always remains a part of your life – your soul – regardless of when you relinquish the juggling ball, whip, or trapeze bar) retire their *circus career* there in order to live in a place that is probably the closest thing to a permanent residence for most, and a place where you know you have *family* around you.

Unlike many who move to Florida's Gulf Coast, circus performers are looking, for the most part in need of, a new job. For the very few that are lucky, a career.

I had been fortunate to have been financially "successful" during my years of performing, but in truth one does not become a "millionaire" (or *anywhere* close to it) when one dedicates their life to the circus and its relevant alternative venues. Of course there are the rare exceptions as with any profession, but if I were to point out the successes of the rare standing artists in Vegas compared to myself, another entertainer could just as easily point out the success of *The Yong Brothers* as compared to their own lives which were just as entrenched in the circus for as many, if not more (not *that* many), years.

So I left one audience, one theater, behind for a totally new audience: the members of the Sheriff's Department and the inmates who past through the jail. Ironically, a lot of my attributes on stage manifested themselves in my new career.

Before I proceed let me assist those who have run out of fingers and toes; I was forty-six when I joined the Sherriff's office.

I was one of the latter of the previously mentioned. It was not a job; it was a career that garnered the same commitment as all I had ever undertaken.

After *thousands* of hours of training throughout my life, the physical prowess necessary for my position was never in question, in fact no where near as demanding; the mental alertness needed to constantly deal with the situations that could – and did – arise in the Sheriff's office (more specifically the jail where I eventually became Shift Commander) required the same (in truth more) focus than was needed for balancing on a ledge twenty stories above ground; and as ironic as it sounds, the interpersonal skills I had developed transacting with thousands of workmen, performers, and audiences (of all different cultures and nationalities) became my true asset when relating with future (and often past) prisoners…also of many different cultures and nationalities.

While I am sure my physical *capabilities* might have been the first thing that future inmates were aware of, it was the way in which I interacted with those that I had incarcerated that gained me the respect to a point that they would even say hello to me when I encountered them on the street – in between their sentences. I would be at fault to not acknowledge that my physical appearance (*a five foot six man with an intimidating physical appearance* -- okay ability to use it) added *somewhat* to my *relationship* with offenders. Not to be remiss, I was also quite fortunate to have a wonderful rapport with my fellow officers, comrades and superiors alike.

Arriving in Sarasota, even with what could be considered a decent savings, was far from satisfactory when you are buying a home, in need of two cars…and caring for an ill child on a twelve thousand dollar a year salary. I am not stoic, of course a part of me clearly remembered what an engagement at *Radio City* paid, but that was the past and the present was all that concerned me.

While some might not be, I am proud to say that I took many part-time jobs just to ensure that my family survived. Considering my childhood, survival might seem like a far from appropriate word, but taking care of your family is survival; in any situation and at all costs.

If my son needed a new wheelchair I was proud, privileged to be able to, stock shelves if that is what it took.

Let me be clear here. I was forty-six and I was beginning anew like a young man ready to conquer the world. I was not *settling*. I began one life performing anywhere they would allow me and sharing my accommodations with fleas before I made it to Vegas and Monte Carlo, I was doing it again. My fortune cookie for the moment: if you can do something once, you can do it again.

I cannot recall how many times I had to fix Tyrone's electric wheelchair, due to simple malfunctions or the unnecessary cruelty of children who thought it would be "cool" to see what happens when tacks are placed in front of the wheels of a wheelchair carrying a helpless boy, but when my frustrations (translated "capabilities") faltered I *often* brought the chair to *Medical Discount Supply* owned by Tom Kruse.

On the fourth or fifth (hundredth) time I arrived with my chair I approached Tom about working there. I mean if I was there so often anyway, why not? While he was not in a position to hire me, I took it upon myself to say I would work for free (this is the time for those young men who want to conquer the world to take notice) till on one day a customer was so impressed by the

A Balanced Life

renovation work I had achieved on a chair that Tom hired me.

I loved my job with the Sheriff's Department, but I had no desire or intention to spend my life in "survival mode" and it was thanks to Tom, one of the most ambitious men I have ever met, that my life really took *balance*. (I've been waiting for a chance to say that.)

It was due to the constant problems and limitations that Tyrone faced with his wheelchair that Tom eventually went on to invent the *Hoveround*, a vehicle that could safely accommodate the large and often hard-to-maneuver places that power wheelchairs which were currently available could not. In essence this man, the man I am proud to call my friend, revolutionized the principles of the power wheelchair while I was working with him, and I cannot imagine how many people – *children* – that his garage creation has helped, not to mention me personally.

It was literally in no time that I was offered the position of Assistant Bureau Commander within the Sheriff's office, and the offer and its realization of future possibilities was what fueled my transformation from a *job* to *career*; a second career after forty-six years.

As you must have thought, the performer in me, the man who loved to challenge the world (himself) physically and mentally, had not died out; it only took on new meaning.

In 1986, with no actual forethought, I entered the Police Olympics in the power lifting competition. I had been *lifting* my brother, and earlier my sister as well, for three-plus decades – what's a little iron. I was mistaken by a *little* iron.

I won *twenty-five gold medals* for power lifting commencing in 1971 when I, in 2006 at seventy-one, after having broke the state record and the national record, broke the *world* record for power lifting; and if you forgive me for jumping ahead, I am *still* winning gold medals (and not in the senior class) till this day.

I attribute Sarasota for this. First it makes me into a winning bodybuilder and now an Olympian; an amazing town.

I stress that, all else aside, I was, am, and always will be an entity of the circus. I am a member of the circus family as they were, are, and always will be of mine. To say it is a part of my soul is too banal, it is at the core of my soul. I am an acrobat who is an official in the Sherriff's Department. I am in no way being superfluous when I say I take the position just as serious (or value it as much) as the circus, but that (the circus) is a part of me that will always be *the* part of me.

And thus it was when I was honored by *my* family.

Sartasota is indisputably the circus capital of the world. The place where young performers aspire to spend their winters and "*older*" ones set up home in when they leave the circus to be close to *their* family.

At St. Armands Circle, in the heart of Sarasota and only feet from the beach, lays the "*Ring of Fame.*" What the *Hollywood Walk of Stars* is to actors and all in the movie industry, the *Ring of Fame* is to the circus; a tribute to honor the greats of *our* industry.

On January 24, 1998 abutting the bronze statue of John Ringling and not far from the plagues to immortalize the talents of Emmett Kelly and Lou Jacobs (but a few of the select honored) *The Yong Brothers* received the honor and I seriously doubt even Betty Grable immortalizing her calves in front of *Grumman's Chinese Theatre* felt the elation that I felt. For the plaque? No. For being recognized, *applauded*, by my lifelong peers.

However, this was not my only tribute to the circus. I should clarify by saying a tribute *I paid* to what the circus and those supported it had done throughout my life. As it turned out, the reward I received was just as great as my initial reasons for offering tribute. From early in my career I had played at *Shrine Circuses* throughout the country. In addition Tyrone, like many unfortunate children, was the recipient of all that the *Shriners* offer to children beset by ailments.

On November eleventh, 1997 I joined the Masons and on June twelfth, 1998 I was given the privilege of becoming a *Shriner* at the Sarasota Shrine Center, of being a member of the organization that had been a valued part of my life, of my son's life.

Now, at seventy-five, with over forty-five years of the circus behind me and over thirty years with the Sherriff's Department, I look at the brochures and posters I have that highlighted my career, my life, around the world; straighten my uniform and get ready for another day as Lieutenant Jonny Yong, and I wonder to myself, "What do I want to do next?"

"Few of us write great novels; all of us live them"

~Mignon McLaughlin~

Epilogue

"Life is a ticket to the greatest show on earth."

~Martin H. Fischer~

MANY PEOPLE, WHEN THEY HAVE REACHED *MY AGE*, spend their days, and countless sleepless nights with questions echoing in their minds. Should I have done this, what if I had, did I really need to, and thousands of other questions (or are they statements?) that have them reflecting on what could have, or should have, been.

A lot of those questions elude me as I spent my life in the center ring, maybe not always in front of actual applauding audiences, but I have treated every moment of life with the dedication of being in the center ring.

And what is the center ring but the chance to bring smiles, breathe life into your audience.

Thus for me I am always in the center ring, because the most important audience I have been blessed to bring smiles to is my family.

But I am no different from most of my counterparts as I too

spend my evenings tossing and turning; but with only one question, one that makes me vastly different from my counterparts.

What do I want to be when I grow up?

> *"Here is the test to find whether your mission on earth is finished. If you're alive, it isn't."*
>
> ~Richard Bach~

Appendix

IN A CAREER THAT HAS SPANNED OVER FOUR DECADES AND three continents Johnny Yong, either performing with *The Yong Sisters and Brothers, The Yong Brothers and Sister* or *The Yong Brothers*, has been *featured* under the spotlight with the greatest circuses in the world, in the world's most majestic venues, and alongside the most renowned talent from the circus, stage, and screen.

* Circus Krone (Germany)
* Cirque Bouglione (France)
* Circus Knie (Switzerland)
* Circus Grock (Germany)
* Circus Schumann (Denmark)
* Circus Barum (Germany)
* Bertram Mills Circus (United Kingdom)
* Ringling Brothers (United States)
* Circo Americano (Spain)
* Circus Scott (Sweden)
* Circus Benneweis (Denmark)

- Festival International Du Cirque Monte Carlo (Monaco)
- Circus Medrano (Italy)
- Circus AMAR (France)
- Black Tower Circus (Scotland)
- Le Lido de Paris (France)
- Moulin Rouge (France)
- Theatre Bobino (France)
- Theatre de l'A,B,C (France)
- Gaumont Palace de Paris (France)
- Casino de Charbonnier (France)
- Estoril Casino (Portugal)
- Casino Wiesbaden (Germany)
- Casino di Campione (Italy)
- Olympia Theater (France)
- Night Club Baccarat (Persia {Iran})
- Casino Travemünde (Germany)
- Theatre de Etoile (France)
- Casino du Liban (Lebanon)
- Africana Club (Italy)
- Circus Circus (Unites States)
- Radio City Music Hall (United States)
- The Savoy (England)
- Roseland (United States)
- Cabaret de Monte Carlo (Monaco)

A Balanced Life

- Phantasialand (Germany)
- Harlem Globetrotters' World Tour
- Holiday on Ice, US Tour
- Bob Hope's USO Tour
- Approximately 1,672 other cabarets, night clubs, hotels, casinos, fairs…and beaches

For those not fortunate enough to see Johnny Yong perform live, he has also been a guest on television programs throughout the United States and Europe:

- The Ed Sullivan Show
- The Dean Martin Show
- The Arthur Godfrey Show
- The Carole Burnett Show
- Super Circus Sealtest Ice Cream with Jerry Colonia
- Hollywood Palace
- Guest performances on over twenty-five programs throughout the 1960's and 1970's
- Nationally run television in France, Germany, Denmark, Holland, Spain, England, and Russia
- And of course…YouTube

NUITS GENEVOISES
D'étonnants équilibristes

Les Young Brothers constituent un monument dans le monde du cirque. Ils ont d'ailleurs le physique de leur prestige. Johnny, 46 ans, a 88 kilos, son frère Walter, 41 ans, 67 kg. Ils ont environ trente ans de cirque et de music-hall derrière eux. Ce duo d'équilibristes américains s'est déjà produit chez Knie en 1951. Ils étaient alors enfants.

Les Young sont chez Maxim's tous les soirs.

C'est une certitude, les Young Brothers figurent parmi les meilleurs équilibristes du monde. Certains de leurs exploits sont même inégalés (notre photo Interpresse). Courez les voir, car les deux hommes vont bientôt quitter le métier. A 45 ans, l'heure de la retraite est proche, si l'on veut s'en aller en ne laissant que des regrets derrière soi. Avant d'entrer sur scène, les Young s'échauffent une demi-heure, car dès le début du numéro, leurs muscles sont mis à rude épreuve. Voici quelques exemples.

Johnny fait la colonne droite sur ses deux mains. Son frère se hisse sur lui et prend appui sur ses pieds. Walter exécute aussi la colonne droite au-dessus de son frère. Johnny marche alors sur le sol en portant son partenaire. Réflexion de Johnny. « Dans une posture comme celle-ci mieux vaut marcher que rester en place. En se déplaçant on trouve toujours moyen de rétablir un équilibre défaillant. Immobiles, il faut tout de suite trouver le juste équilibre et le conserver. Sinon, c'est la chute.»

Second exploit des Young. Johnny se met en équilibre sur la tête. Son frère se hisse sur lui et se met, lui aussi, en chandelle sur la tête. Son crâne reposant sur la plante des pieds de Johnny. Cet équilibre est extrêmement difficile à conserver. Tout l'édifice humain repose sur Johnny. « A ce moment un rien peut me gêner, par exemple, des vibrations trop importantes provenant de l'orchestre.»

Au final, le frère aîné se hisse sur une main. Walter prend appui sur la nuque de Johnny. Les deux hommes écartent ensuite jambes et bras de façon à former deux X superposés. Du grand art, sans artifice. Les Young Brothers sont vraiment des superstars.

Michel BAETTIG

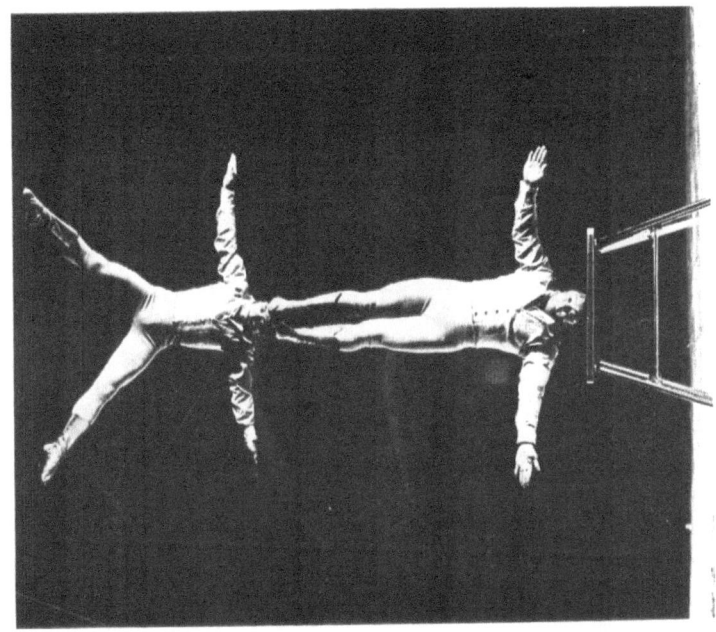

Verdens bedste håndstand

»Young Brothers« i deres fantastiske nummer

TV's cirkuseksprt, programsekretær Kurt Møller Madsen, har set på cirkus i Jernbanegade i København. Han er faldet for de to artister Walther og Johnny Young, der laver et af Cirkus Benneweis' mest fantastiske numre, håndstandsnummeret. Artisterne — der med et vanskeligt ord kaldes håndstandsekvilibrister — har som de eneste uden for Sovjetunionen modtaget den russiske artistmedalje i guld for deres fabelagtige præstationer.

I udsendelsen fortælles om, hvordan det enestående nummer, der regnes for det bedst udførte i verden, er blevet til. »Young Brothers« er henholdsvis 31 og 33 år, og de har arbejdet med deres nummer siden de var otte og ti år. De er de højest betalte håndstandsekvilibrister i verden.

Dansk TV kl. 20,00

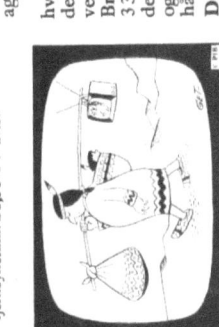

Johnny Yong

De er verdens dygtigste på deres felt - men der er

KOLDT PÅ TOPPEN ISÆR NÅR MAN STÅR PÅ HÆNDER

Young Brothers, internationalt artistpar, blev taget på ordet: De måtte gøre deres nummer på toppen af SAS-hotellet i København - og klarede det. Og så gav de bagefter et par ekstranumre

AF OTTO LUDWIG
Fot. Per Wilmann

SØNDAG 10. MAJ

SØNDAGS-AKTUEL

A Balanced Life

En dobbelt håndstand højt over byens toge. Du blev blæst ned at par gange - men heldigvis ikke ned på gaden 22 etager nede...

■ De er verdens dygtigste på dette felt. Alligevel står de med begge hænder på jorden. De kan dog også nøjes med at stå på den ene. Og de behøver ikke engang at stå på jorden. De kan gøre det hvor som helst.

– Endog på kanten af Royal Hotel, sagde de en aften i Cirkus Benneweis' kantine.

Vi tog dem på ordet, og de tog os med storm. Job, vist blæste de Vinden var så kraftig, at Young Brothers var omtrent lige så bange vi eksperimentet som vi selv.

22 etager til vejrs

Da lillebror Walther skulle op at stå på fødderne af storebror Johnny, mens denne selv stod på hænder, faldt de ned flere gange. Heldigvis faldt de ikke ned på gaden 22 etager nede. Kun ned på hotellets tag.

Young Brothers er amerikanske statsborgere. Men de er født i Tyskland. Deres forældre, som selv har været akrobater, er på mødrende side tysk og på fædrende kinesisk.

Begge begyndte deres artist-karriere, da de var fem år. Engang optrådte hele familien samlet. – Johnny har gået i skole både i Tyskland, Frankrig og England. – Han var skolens dygtigste i gymnastik, men den dårligste i matematik.

De træner næsten aldrig

Det nummer, brødrene viser i København gamle cirkusbygning, har de haft sammen i 25 år. De træner næsten ikke. Men Johnny, der med sine knapt 35 år er den ældste og kraftigste, fungerer som undermand – derfor må han nu og da træne sine halsmuskler op. Det gør han ved at stå på hovedet en halv time ad gangen. Hans muskler er som ædt at føle på.

Med begge hænder på jorden passerer artisterne ver mest bange for at blive trådt ned af fodgængerne...

Johnny Young sagde efter præstationen på toppen af Royal Hotel, at skulle være. Jeg kan ikke tale med om det. Jeg turde slet ikke se den ikke havde været helt, som den det.

Preview of 'Holiday on Ice' promises much for GR audiences next week

by David Nicolette

LANSING — Holiday on Ice this year schedules its appearance in Grand Rapids at the very start of the holiday season, opening on Wednesday, the day before Thanksgiving, and offering nine performaces through Sunday.

It's perfect timing for a show that regularly takes its production number themes from the holidays, but a bit difficult from the standpoint of reviewing the show opening night. Since the troupe was in Lansing this week, and the Civic Center there isn't too different from Civic Auditorium in Grand Rapids, a preview appeared the best way of handling it.

This particular edition of Holiday on Ice is its 25th Anniversary special, and the overall production matches the challenge of the event in exceptional lighting and costuming, some really entertaining specialty acts and outstanding dance-skate routines by at least two of the principals.

—Grand Rapids Press Photograph
The Yong Brothers Balance on a Moving Car

Less Impressive

Less impressive was the ensemble work of the chorus skaters, though part of the fault may have been the fairly bad accompaniment by the orchestra made up primarily of Lansing musicians.

Much of the music is taped, and that came off well, but this is supplemented by the work of eight or ten live players. The orchestra was overly loud, and the brass, taxed by repeated demands for fanfares and finely timed attacks, was ragged and often off key.

Past years have proved the pickup band in Grand Rapids to be much more skillful, so the chorus work, if the accompaniment affected the performance, may come off better.

More Demanding

The choreography, incidentally, makes more demands on the chorus for individual steps and movement than the show normally does, and this may have something to do with the feeling of disruption of smooth flow expected of group skating.

In one number, however, there was no such difficulty. That one is called "Fourth of July" and is lively, has beautiful costumes, includes the traditional pinwheel and shows the young chorus skaters at their best.

Among the principals the best is Jimmie Crockett, who appears in three numbers but is particularly striking in his interpretation of the opera clown Pagliacci, in a number titled "Salute to the Operas." He employs all his skills as skater, dancer and mime.

Adagio Team Good

Carol and Clive Phipson, the show's husband and wife adagio team, are among the best performers in the show

handsome pair. Add to that a smoothness of maneuvers and their difficult lifts, balances and perfect poses in motion appear so effortless that all the beauty may be enjoyed without even a thought of mishap.

For comedy, Little Lido is marvelous as "A Latin Madcap," and in another number called "The Mad, Mod World of April Fools," a treat for adults and children. His timing, both as a skater and pantomime comedian, is a joy to watch.

Little Lido does get some strong competition from Werner and Denise Muller and their Holiday Chimps. The chimpanzees are hilarious: really performers unmatched by any other such animal act in memory. They do all their routines on skates and are as agile as humans. One very strange sight is a chimp skating as a human, playing the part of a bull in a bullfight ring. Any aficionado will roll in the aisles at this one.

Routines Funny

Lance Shinkle and Jim McGlocklin have a couple of pretty funny comedy routines, complete with speed skating and near misses plus threats from the water bucket.

A couple of outstanding acts which aren't generally expected in an ice show are the Yong brothers, a remarkable balancing team which performs on the top of a moving car, and Tommy Curtin, a juggler who manages to keep several objects in the air while skating smoothly. He was with the show in Grand Rapids several years ago and repeats a very clever stick juggling routine which is beautifully timed and rhythmic as well.

One of the young skaters who is fast numbers is performed with a new partner, a very skilled Linda Adams, who is making her first tour with this contingent of the Holiday troupes. (There are two in the United States and four in other parts of the world.)

Other women skaters are attractive and effective in various numbers: Roberta Laurent, Sandy Wirwill, Brigitte V and the comely Daly Tripletts.

Ol' Houn' Dawg is back with some new stuff, proving you can teach an old dog new tricks. The Averys do their nostalgic waltz routines with a couple of snappy new little maneuvers.

A summary must include the report that Holiday on Ice remains a show for the whole family.

A Balanced Life

ILLUSTRERET Familie Journal
Nr. 26 . 30. juni 1970 . 94. årgang . Kr. 2,40

Verdensnummeret Young Brothers, som Kurt Møller Madsen præsenterer os for. Brødrene er internationalt berømte og sikkert cirkus' dyreste nummer

I CIRKUS med TV

Fire verdensnumre — og hvordan de er blevet til

Cirkus er godt fjernsynsstof, specielt når det er lagt i hænderne på Kurt Møller Madsen. Han er netop færdig med en ny serie, som præsenteres de kommende fire lørdage under titlen »Et nummer«. Hos Cirkus Benneweis har han fundet fire numre, som han skildrer sammen med fotografen Ib Skov. Det bliver først Young Brothers, og siden skal vi også se babyelefanterne, hvis opvækst og dressur Møller Madsen har fulgt. Og så skal vi møde pauseklovnerne Jackie, Antonio og Little Billy. Filmene er i farver, og man følger et nummer fra det bygges op, til det udfolder sig festligt i projektørernes skær i manegen. Det er gjort så dokumentarisk som muligt. Ib Skov har gået med kameraet fastklemt på skulderen hele tiden for at følge de medvirkende privat, i garderoben og på scenen. Udsendelserne er på en måde en fortsættelse af de populære Cirkus ABCer, men alligevel adskiller de sig fra de tidligere produktioner. Senere på sommeren får vi mere TV-cirkus. Kurt Møller Madsen er nu i gang med en stor udsendelse med titlen »Cirkusbygningen«.

Un autre cliché de cette page vous montre trois petits Chinois exécutant un exercice demandant un sens de l'équilibre très poussé. Cette fois, ils ne sont plus que deux à effectuer des prouesses et l'on conviendra en voyant nos deux acrobates qu'ils ont plus d'un tour dans leur sac. Admirez l'aisance avec laquelle ils se tiennent en équilibre. Le parallélisme de leurs mouvements est tout bonnement surprenant et nous nous demandons combien d'heures de répétition il leur a fallu pour arriver à ce résultat.

Circus Bouglione
Belgium
Bruxelles
1950.

Les acrobates chinois défient toutes les lois de l'équilibre.

A Balanced Life

EKSTRA BLADET, Copenhagen

www.ingramcontent.com/pod-product-compliance
Ingram Content Group UK Ltd.
Pitfield, Milton Keynes, MK11 3LW, UK
UKHW041950230426
12048UKWH00008B/251